D0842131

Hellsing d20 system

Written by Michelle Lyons and Adam Jury with Mark C. MacKinnon
d20 System Material by Matthew Keeley
Edited by Mark C. MacKinnon, Editing Assistance by Amy Restemayer
Designed by Jeff Mackintosh, Graphic Production by Adam Jury
Production Assistance by Karen A. McLarney

HELLSING © 2002 Kouta Hirano • SHONEN GAHOSHA Co., LTD / Hellsing K.G.
GUARDIANS OF ORDER, BESM d20 and TRI-STAT SYSTEM are trademarks of Guardians Of Order, Inc.

'D20 SYSTEM' and the 'D20 SYSTEM' logo are Trademarks owned by Wizards of the Coast and are used according to the terms of the d20 System License version 6.0. A copy of this license can be found at www.wizards.com/d20.

DUNGEONS & DRAGONS® and Wizards of the Coast® are Registered Trademarks of Wizards of the Coast, and are used with Permission.

Copyright © 2004 Guardians Of Order, Inc. / GENEON ENTERTAINMENT (USA) INC.

All rights reserved under international law. No part of this book may be reproduced in part or in whole, in any form or by any means, without permission from the publisher, except for brief quotes for use in reviews.

First Printing — July 2004 Printed in China

Guardians Of Order, Inc.
P.O. Box 25016
370 Stone Road
Guelph, Ontario
CANADA N1G 4T4

Phone: 519-821-7174
Fax: 519-821-7635

info@guardiansorder.com
http://www.guardiansorder.com

ISBN 1-894938-45-3
Product Number 02-672

HELLSING

The *Hellsing* anime series is based upon the *manga* series of the same name by Kouta Hirano. The *manga* is published by Monthly Young King Ours and Shonen Gahosha Co., LTD. The series was produced in Japan by Studio Gonzo and licensed to Pioneer Entertainment (USA) Inc. — now GENEON ENERTAINMENT (USA) INC. — for American release.

Hellsing was designed as a limited run series, 13 episodes in length. It originally aired weekly on Fuji Television starting October 10, 2001 in the 2:25 AM to 2:50 AM timeslot due to the show's violent content and adult themes. A boxed set containing all thirteen episodes on four DVDs was released in April 2003. This book deals with characters, world and story presented in all 13 seven episodes.

Hellsing is set in a horrific version of the modern world where undead walk the night in search of blood and power. The time frame is current-day England, with a focus on London. The primary emphasis of the series is the Hellsing Organisation — a secret group working with the English government to keep the undead menace in hand.

The primary character of the series is Arucard, a supposedly ancient vampire who works with the Hellsing Organisation to destroy lesser members of his own kind. His name is a veiled reference to Dracula, the vampire from Bram Stoker's novel of the same name, published in 1897.

SUPERNATURAL ACTION GENRE

Hellsing is definitely in the supernatural action family of anime. There are elements of horror in the vampires and ghouls that stalk the night, killing innocents and corrupting the countryside. This series shows some differences from others in the same style in that the heroes *are* the same type of creatures they face and destroy on a nightly basis. In addition, there are supernatural and technological elements at work, with aspects of supernatural horror (vampirism, undeath, regeneration, etc.) duplicated by technology — usually to the detriment of all.

Other series in this genre include:
Vampire Hunter D (1985)
3x3 Eyes (1991)
Devil Man (1987)
Judge (1991)
SoulTaker (2001)
BioHunter (1995)
Vampire Hunter D: Bloodlust (2000)
Wicked City (1987)
Blood: The Last Vampire (2000)
Demon City Shinjuku (1988)
Vampire Princess Miyu (1988)

Opening Credits

Based on the comic by	Kouta Hirano
Series Publisher	Monthly Young King Ours Shonen Gahosha Co., LTD.
Animation Planned by	Pioneer LDC Gonzo
Executive Producers	Yasuyuki Ueda (Pioneer LDC) Showji Murahama (Gonzo)
Supervising Producer	Yoshiyuki Fudetani (Shonen Gahosha Co., LTD.)
Director	Yasunori Urata
Screenwriter	Chiaki J. Konaka
Character Designs	Toshiharu Murata
Mechanical Designs	Yoshitaka Kono
Art Director	Shinji Katahira
Colour Designer	Keiko Kai
VFX Director	Atsushi Takeyama
Digital Editors	Kengo Shigemura Ryuta Muranaka
Music	Yasushi Ishii
Sound Director	Yota Tsuruoka
TV Producer	Daisuke Kawakami Fuji Television
Production Studios	Gonzo/Digimation
Supervising Director	Umanosuke Iida
Produced by	Hellsing K.G. Fuji Television

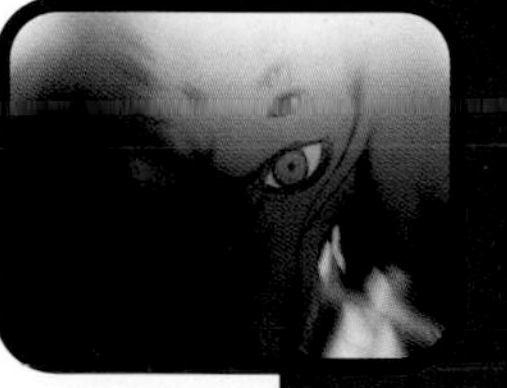

Hellsing

Episode Summaries

In the name of God, impure souls of the living dead shall be banished into eternal damnation. Amen.

— Title screen of Hellsing

The *Hellsing* series is an amasing addition to the body of vampire-based literature, film and television programs already in existence. The anime is beautifully drawn, with the subtle use of computer animation adding unexpected depth and realism to the stunning artwork. The impressive visuals, however, are not the only high-quality mark of the show.

Over the past decade or so, the vampire has made a resounding rebound into popular culture. The novels by Anne Rice and the subsequent films *Interview with a Vampire* and *Queen of the Damned*, the role-playing game *Vampire: The Masquerade* by White Wolf, and the television series *Forever Knight*, *Buffy the Vampire Slayer*, and *Angel* are all evidence of North America's fascination with the vampire and its primordial lusts.

The *Hellsing* series adds to that impressive litany of popular culture with a twist; here it is the vampire who culls its own herd. Instead of spreading death and unnatural appetites throughout the world, the ancient vampire seeks to destroy them, aiding the descendant of his old enemy by fighting against a new threat created by the humans themselves: a technological vampire, living beyond the threshold of death and revelling in its monstrous new status.

This shifting of perspectives and loyalties is examined throughout the series, most obviously in the case of Officer Seras Victoria, a police officer embraced — turned into a vampire — by Arucard in the first episode. Seras serves as an "everyman" figure for the show and is used as a point of reference for the viewer. The changes she goes through in both her daily life (or unlife, as you prefer) as well as her relationship with, and growing understanding of the dark world around her serve as an obvious focal point to the murkier themes playing out in the rest of the story.

Hellsing is set in modern day England. The lack of cultural o date references makes it almost impossible to tell exactly when it is set, but the overall level o technology is roughly equivalent to our own (perhaps even a few years in the future). The story follows the members of a group called the Hellsing Organisation in their search for the makers and distributors of the Freak chip — an implanted microchip that turns humans into vampires.

Hellsing

Episode: 01

Order 01: The Undead

The episode opens on a night in London. Three black military helicopters track a Jaguar through the streets of London to a large manor house. An older man and a young woman go into the house, where the man begins caressing the woman's body.

A man dressed in red steps out of the shadows of the room, interrupting them. He draws a silver gun and points it at the pair, then shoots the woman as the older man shrinks back. The woman's body turns to dust as it hits the floor. When the older man looks around for her assailant, the man in red is gone.

Outside, military vehicles and troops surround the house. The man in red walks up to a car and reports that the mission is accomplished before walking out the gates and into the night.

Sometime later, two men and a woman sit watching a tape of strange dogs eating human remains, followed by the picture of a strange vampiric priest. The older of the men explains that the village of Cheddar has been experiencing a wave of missing persons ever since this priest was assigned there. The regular police forces were killed trying to investigate, and so the elite unit D-11 had been sent in. Half of that unit has also been killed.

The woman, Sir Integra Hellsing, appears both amused and bored by this explanation. She cuts the man off and

upbraids him for not following the proper procedure, namely calling in the Hellsing Organisation to deal with the problem. She explains that she already has an agent on the way.

The scene changes to Cheddar, where wounded figures lie crumpled on the ground. One of the D-11 officers, Seras Victoria, is unhurt and rushing first aid to another one. She is scared and frightened. Halfway through treating her companion, the officer changes, sitting up, growling and lunging at her. Although her teammate has the appearance of a corpse, she cannot bring herself to shoot him. Seras hits him with the grip of her gun and runs back to the vehicle. She discovers that all her wounded or killed fellow officers are now up and walking, afflicted with the same condition as her friend. She fires her gun and hits, but the ghoul is unaffected. She runs into the woods to escape them.

Seras stops in a clearing, out of breath. A ghoulish woman soon approaches her through the trees. Seras struggles to shoot, when suddenly an arm appears in the middle of the ghoul's chest. The ghoul screams and bursts, falling into dust. The man in red stands smiling behind the ghoul. The man seems amused by Seras's actions and tells her it's a beautiful night, "if you're a bloodsucker." Seras shoots him in the shoulder, a wound that heals instantly. She panics and runs away while the man in red laughs.

It is a short time later when Seras finds herself in an unfamiliar part of the forest. She is lost and confused with nowhere to go when she realises that she's on the edge of a graveyard. Across the yard is a church, with lights flickering inside. Seras goes to it in search of safety.

As Seras enters, she draws her weapon. A priest steps into the light and greets her, walking up to the podium. His manner of speaking is friendly, but odd. She is confused, since she was sent to deal with a priest, but she cannot reconcile his appearance with the inhuman monsters outside. He explains that the monsters outside are ghouls, undead slaves of the vampire who created them. He then hypnotises Seras and levitates her toward him, telling her that she'll be a wonderful vampire.

Seras lifts her gun to the priest's head by sheer force of will and threatens to blow his brains out if he doesn't let her go. The priest ignores her, confident in his power over her. Before he can bend and bite her neck, though, the doors burst open. The man in red stands there.

The man introduces himself as Arucard, a servant of the Hellsing

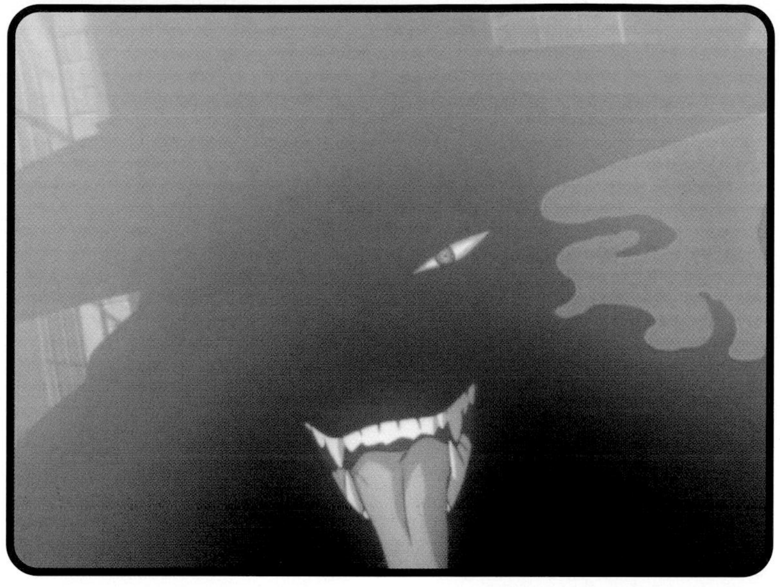

Organisation. Angered, the priest signals his minions and orders them to kill Arucard. Dozens of ghouls stand up in the pews armed with guns. Arucard ignores them and continues walking toward the priest, spouting insults. The ghouls open fire on Arucard, reducing him to little more than a bloody wreck on the floor of the church. The priest snaps his fingers and the shooting stops.

The priest is about to turn his attention back to Seras when Arucard's body begins to rise, pulling itself back together in a black mist. The priest panics as he realises that Arucard is a vampire as well. He tells the ghouls to shoot again, but Arucard is too quick.

Arucard pulls his gun and kills the ghouls quickly, taking out multiple targets with a single shot. The priest panics. He tries to talk Arucard into joining forces with him, abandoning the Hellsing Organisation. Arucard ignores his entreaties.

In desperation, the priest uses Seras as a body shield. Arucard doesn't respond, and the priest goes back to his former tactic of trying to talk Arucard into changing sides. Arucard finally speaks, but only to Seras, ignoring the priest.

Arucard explains that he's going to shoot through Seras to kill the priest, and that this will kill her as well. He offers her the chance to become like him to preserve her existence and she agrees. She chooses to be embraced. Arucard fires, blasting a large hole in Seras and killing the priest. Arucard approaches Seras where she lies on the floor and crouches over her, biting her on the neck. and drinking deeply

A short time later, Arucard appears outside the church, carrying Seras in his arms wrapped in a blanket. He walks over to Integra, who is waiting with a displeased expression, and gives her a status report. Integra criticises his performance and then turns to go. Arucard tells Integra that he wants Seras transferred to the Hellsing Organisation. Integra is angry and accuses him of overstepping his bounds. Arucard replies that Seras made the choice for herself. Integra turns on her heel and leaves, giving the signal for the troops to move out.

Arucard stands alone with Seras. He comments on the beauty of the night, much as he did earlier in the clearing when they met for the first time. He waits for her response. Seras is struck by the irony of the moment and gives a faint smile.

Hellsing

Episode: 02

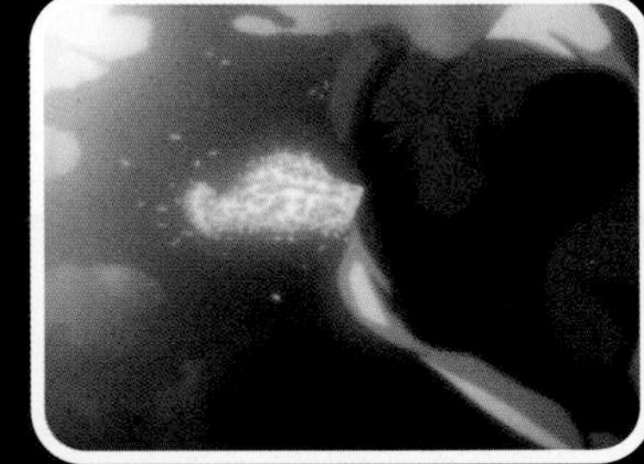

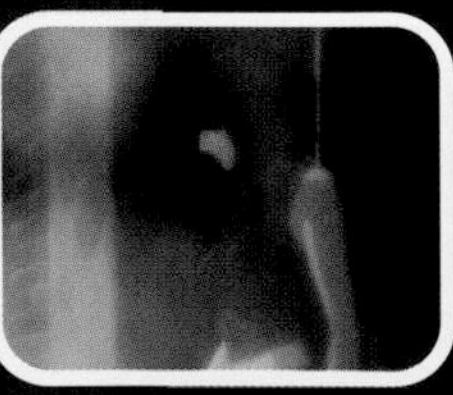

Order 02: Club M

One rainy night in London, a group of friends leave a popular night spot. On a nearby rooftop, Seras sets up a sniper rifle without needing the aid of a scope. An older man dressed in a military uniform with a "Hellsing" insignia accompanies her. As Seras gets into position, one of the women in the group wanders away, toward an alley.

A strange female standing in the alley approaches the woman who seems hypnotised. One of the men from the group joins the woman, breaking the spell. They lose track of the female and are about to leave when she reaches up from the ground and grabs the woman's ankles.

Seras receives the order to shoot but can't bring herself to do it. Another sniper nearby takes the shot and kills the ghoul. Only seconds later can Seras move her finger away from the trigger, disappointed in herself for freezing up under pressure. The rest of unit begin cleaning up the crime scene.

The scene changes briefly to a dark house, the door previously blown open with a shotgun. A children's television program plays in the background. The view cuts back to Hellsing headquarters as the troops are being dismissed following the mission.

Seras's commanding officer calls her over and dresses her down, suggesting that she's unfit for fieldwork. A man who asks for Seras interrupts him. The officer walks away, leaving Seras confused and upset.

The man leads Seras inside the mansion, down stairways and into the depths of the house. He introduces himself as Walter, the retainer of the Hellsing family, and says that he will look after her. Seras is still upset regarding her conversation with the commander, and her attempts at levity fall flat. Walter informs her of the dangers of sunlight and silver to her new existence, leaving her nonplussed. She is shown to her room deep within the house and her convertible four-poster coffin-bed.

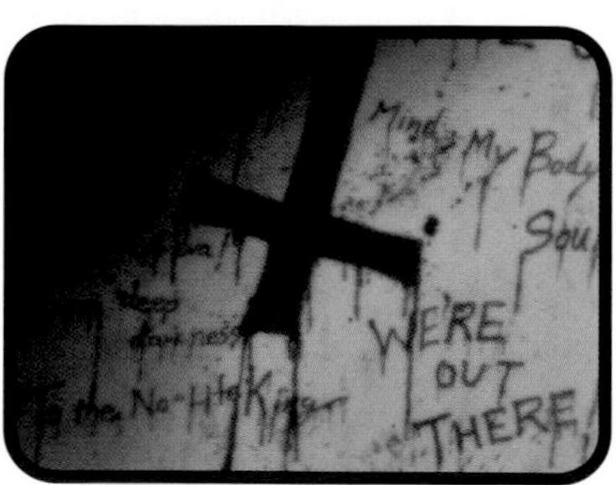

Back at the ransacked house, the walls are covered with graffiti written in blood. The children's program is still playing in the background, but the television has been knocked over and is also covered in blood. Police sirens cut through the air as the units race to the house.

Seras attempts to rest but fails. It is still night-time, and her body will not sleep at night now. She gets up and leaves her room, coming back into the main hall. She sees two doormen, only to be warned by Integra not to feed on them. Seras is indignant, but Integra does not give her a chance to reply before walking away.

Integra walks into her office, where Arucard joins her. She tells him that a group of individuals have been killing entire families near Birmingham, drinking their blood then scrawling blasphemous messages on the walls. Arucard retires until the next night. Seras arrives back in her room to see a bag of blood left for her. She smiles and moves toward it, then realises what she's doing. She knocks the blood off the table, regaining control.

The scene cuts to two teenagers, Lief and Jessica, riding a moped and weaving through traffic, daring other cars to hit them. Soon, they are in a house, where they've killed a family and trashed the room. They kiss and make out, treating their murderous extravaganza as a lark. They note that with nine more victims, they'll be even stronger and can stay young forever. Jessica then performs oral sex on Lief as he unleashes a stream of bullets into the reanimated corpses of his victims.

The next night at the Hellsing training centre, a number of soldiers are on the firing range. Seras joins them, where she's given a huge gun to shoot. She thinks they're playing a joke on her, but finds that she can lift it

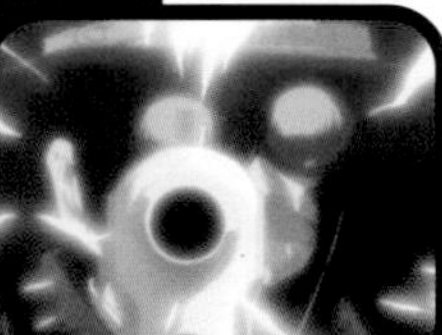

easily. She shoots with it and hits the target, but is told by officer Gareth that her shot is not accurate, since the undead have to be hit in the heart and nowhere else. Seras is annoyed, but has no time to dwell on it as the troops are called into action.

While the troops are deployed, Integra takes a moment for her own target practice; her marksmanship is exceptional. Walter updates her on the blockade that's been established. Integra notes that these vampires seem to have no idea what they've become, only barely touched by the curse. Integra asks Walter if he would want to be out there, but he refutes the idea, instead expressing his satisfaction in serving her.

Jessica and Lief are tearing through the countryside, shooting up

cars and killing policemen. They approach the blockade, heedless of what's ahead. Arucard watches them and activates one of his powers, creating an illusion around them. The two vampires find themselves suddenly lost in a strange and frightening world. Arucard appears in their path, and Lief decides to run him down. Arucard draws his gun and fires, however, knocking them off the moped.

Arucard insults Lief and Jessica as he seemingly teleports around them, provoking Lief to attack. Lief shoots Arucard in the chest, but the Hellsing vampire heals himself and laughs. Arucard fires his pistol at Lief, killing him quickly. Jessica panics and runs away as Arucard drops the illusion, letting her escape for Seras to eliminate.

Jessica runs toward Seras's position as she sits with a sniper rifle at the ready. Her commander, Peter, gives Seras the command to fire but she can't bring herself to do it — she simply cannot get over Jessica's human appearance. It isn't until Gareth says he has acquired the target that Peter's urging gets through to her. She shoots and hits Jessica, who falls to the ground and turns to dust. Peter smiles and welcomes Seras to the Hellsing Organisation.

As the unit prepares to leave, Arucard approaches Seras. He congratulates her on her work, then changes the subject and tells her that she'll never be human again. He tells her to drink the blood, for she will become weak without it. He then vanishes. Seras is angry, but finds herself saying, "Yes, Master," to the night air.

ROLLSROYCE
SILVER CLOUD II
ER
103
POLICE
L703 GYO
エンブレム
VESPA150
モドキ
HELSING
POLICE
HELLSING
兵員輸送車
上面
側面
HELLSING #1
装甲車

Hellsing

EPISODE: 03

ORDER 03: SWORD DANCER

In a Catholic school dormitory, a blond-haired boy named Enrico sits next to his dark-haired friend and lover, Mick, on a bed. Mick is dead, apparently because Enrico drank too much of his blood. Enrico promises Mick that they will be together forever as he leans over to kiss his friend. Before he can do so, however, the door bursts open. A group of men and a priest stand there, shocked at what they see.

The scene cuts to a train from Paris arriving at a London station. A very tall blond man with short hair, glasses, and a priest's robes disembarks from the train. The attendant welcomes him to London, and he gives her a blessing with an amused grin.

Later, in a private hospital autopsy room, Enrico's body is examined. Integra and the local police lieutenant (from the first episode) are watching. As the autopsy progresses, the lieutenant notes that Enrico was a foreign national of noble birth attending college in England. The doctor conducting the autopsy finds a computer chip in the cadaver's neck.

Back in Hellsing mansion, Seras stumbles into her room. She's desperately tired and weak. Seeing the blood that's been left for her, she sits and pours it into a bowl. She cannot bring herself to eat, however, and so pours it down the toilet. As she does

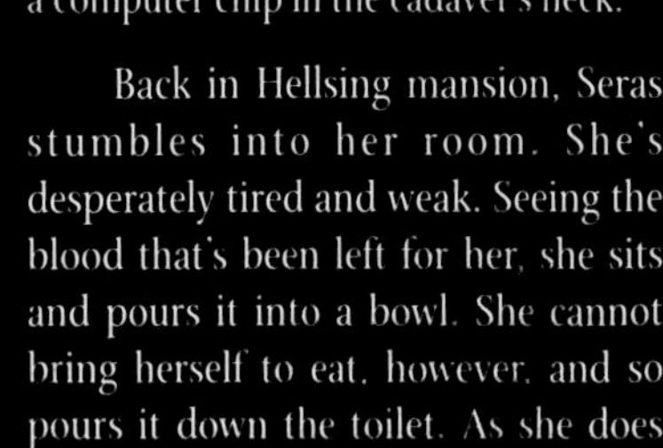

so, Arucard's voice resounds in her head, upbraiding her for her behaviour and telling her that her failure to drink is causing weakness. She leaves the room, bowl in hand, and begins looking for Arucard.

Arucard is in Integra's office, though, as Integra sits contemplating the chip that was removed from Enrico's body. She and Arucard discuss the chip and its implications. Frustrated, she taunts him with being the same as the chipped humans. He levitates the chip as a means of demonstrating the difference, then drops it back down to the table again. Integra apologises and resumes her conversation with Arucard, only to be interrupted by a phone call announcing the arrival of dignitaries to the Hellsing mansion. Arucard is gone by the time she hangs up the phone.

Enrico awakens from a blood haze in a hospital. He is talking to Mick, not realising that his lover is gone. He goes searching, killing everyone who tries to stop him. The policemen arrive and order him to stop but he attacks them too.

Back at Integra's office, the visitors have left. Integra is angry, going over the papers she was given including a picture of the blond priest. She curses the Vatican and the Iscariot Organisation, only to stop suddenly when the phone rings.

A few moments later, Walter and Integra are walking outside the Hellsing Mansion. Walter is apprising Integra on the situation at the hospital. Peter approaches and salutes, telling her that the Hellsing Company A is leaving for the scene. Seras joins the departing troops as Integra watches. Once the units depart, Integra orders Arucard to help as well, despite Walter's disagreement. She insists that England is a Protestant country, and the Vatican will not be allowed free reign.

In the hospital basement, Enrico is killing rampantly while calling for Mick. The Hellsing units arrive and deploy, with Seras carrying the huge gun she was given previously. When they lose contact with the troops that were sent ahead of Gareth and Seras, Gareth realises that the soldiers have been killed. Through the haze of battle, Seras's heightened vision spots Enrico surrounded by reanimated ghouls and calling his lover's name.

As she watches, Arucard speaks to her telepathically from his seat outside the hospital, sipping on a bag of blood. He instructs her to fire at the heart or head only. Seras obeys instantly and kills them. Enrico stumbles out of the passage seconds later, still calling for Mick. Before Seras can pull the trigger Gareth

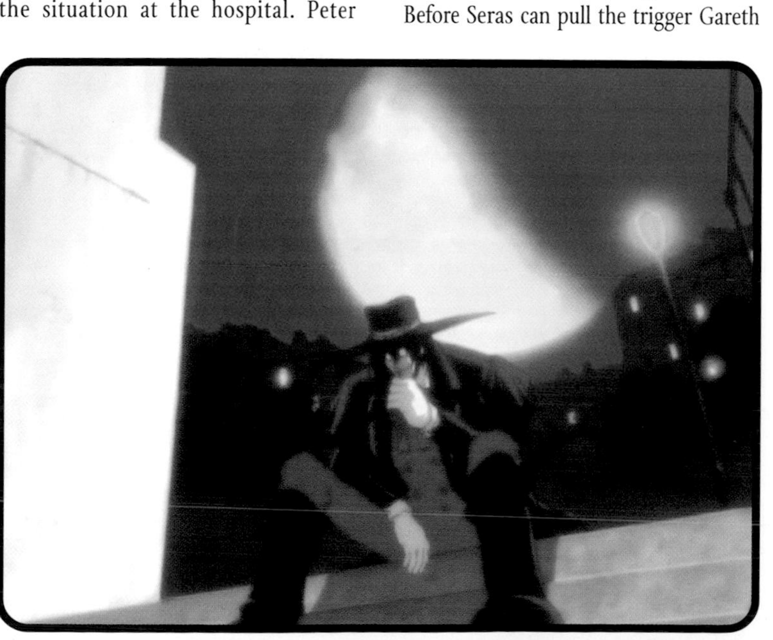

falls dead to the floor in front of her, stabbed in the back.

Seras stands and turns to see who did this, only to catch a sword through her throat. She falls to her knees as the Vatican priest strides forward, condemning her for her vampiric existence. He then heads down the hall, calling himself the "instrument of God." He closes on Enrico with his sword as the mad vampire charges. A moment later, the vampire falls to dust as Arucard impales Enrico on his gloved hand.

Arucard and the priest square off, with Arucard calling him "paladin." The paladin wards the hallway against Arucard's powers, then says a prayer in which he announces his intention to kill Arucard. They attack one another and end in a stalemate, with Arucard's gun at the paladin's head and the paladin's sword in Arucard's stomach. Arucard shoots the priest, knocking him back onto the floor. Arucard turns away then, pulling the blessed blade out of his body and trying to assist Seras to her feet.

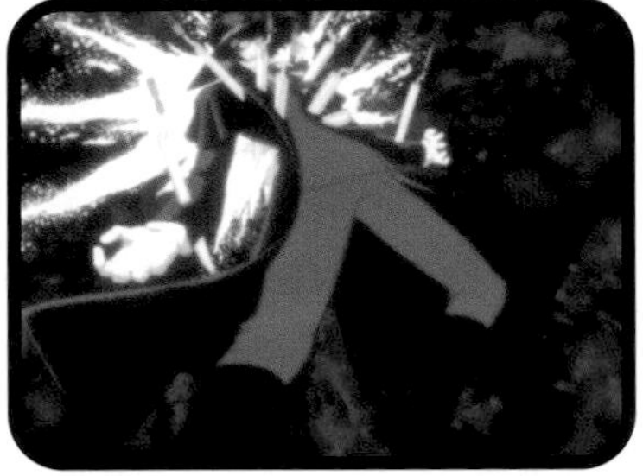

The priest is not dead, however, and sneaks up on Arucard. Seras tries to warn him, but is unable to help. The priest attacks, filling Arucard's body with knives. Arucard realises too late that the priest is a "regenerator," capable of healing even deadly wounds. They stand off, ready to fight again when Integra's voice cuts through the combat, stopping them both. She calls the priest Paladin Alexander Andersong and presents him with his walking papers — an order from Andersong's superior to leave England at once.

The paladin acquiesces with a smug grin, telling Integra that he looks forward to seeing her again. As soon as he leaves, she begins ripping down the warding papers and berating Arucard and Seras for their performances. She leaves then, as Arucard pulls the knives out of himself and Seras. After the last knife is removed, he kneels before her and tells her to drink his blood so that she will no longer be in servitude to him. The vampire part of her nature takes over, anxious for the blood, but she stops herself and pulls back. Arucard stands and begins to fade out of sight. He asks if this is her choice, and she can only say that right now, she's not ready.

SCORPION STYLE
ヤンの銃
P90改
LOCK
HELLSING
MP5A5
HK MP5
Cal.9mm×19
レンズキャップ
※発射中は止まってます。
F.サイト
R.サイト
HELLSING
STEYR MPi81
HELLSING
セラスのライフル
Hellsing
スコーピオン
ルークの銃
cut down M1 Rifle
発火前
発火後
HELLSING
ITHACA
M37
SHOTGUN

Hellsing

Episode: 04

Order 04: Innocent as a Human

The episode opens with an image of a computer screen. A password is being typed in, and an image of a man being shot is played and edited. Elsewhere in London, a shot is fired in a dark apartment on a typical foggy night in the city. In the shadow of a cathedral not far away, the Hellsing troops are out on manoeuvres.

A man named Steadler has replaced Gareth, the unit commander who was killed. As the troops load onto the personnel carrier, he stops Seras and insults her with sexist and degrading comments regarding her vampiric nature.

The scene changes to Integra's office, where she's talking to Peter about Steadler. After they finish talking, Integra meets with Walter, who shows her the video file from the opening scene. He tells her that he found it on the Internet marketed as a snuff video. Walter zooms in on the image of the dead man, showing a Hellsing badge on the victim's uniform.

Walter indicates that it seems to have been recorded during an incident in Coventry three weeks previous. A local TV news station is already trying to investigate the clip. Walter tells Integra

that he's arranging for the Ministry of Media Management to kill the story and destroy all related information. Integra seconds these actions, intent that the innocent masses never find out about the Hellsing Organisation.

Back with Seras and Steadler, the troops are raiding a building in Camden where a stash of illegal small arms has been found along with evidence of ghoul activity. As they deploy, Steadler picks on Seras and tells her to go in first.

Integra hangs up the phone, saying that MI-5 has already begun dealing with the information leak. Arucard phases in during this conversation and asks Walter for a new, larger gun. Walter says he has something in mind, and Arucard turns to leave. Integra asks Arucard for his help, but he turns her down, saying that there's nothing he can do to help.

A short time later, Walter shows Integra a news report on television, showing the operation the troops are on at the moment. Integra heads to the scene and watches the news program on the way. The reporter, Kim, is the woman who was attacked by a ghoul in Episode Two. She is struck by how audacious the reporter is and how much damage this could be doing. She wonders who is behind this leak, just as Walter tells her that the station has been ordered to cease the broadcast.

Seras and her unit are searching the building. They find a number of dead ghouls, with blood everywhere. She kills one that attacks her unit, then reports that the rest are entrenched on the third floor. Steadler tells her that he has it covered; gunshots from above follow shortly. Peter then radios Seras with a job for her to do. Soon, night-enhanced footage shows Seras walking through the building, alone. She hears a scream in a room and bursts in, finding a man lying on the ground, crying, amid overturned computer equipment. The man is taken into custody. Afterwards, Seras confronts Steadler, asking him how he knew that the targets were waiting on the third floor and why he didn't tell the forward unit. He smirks and ignores her questions, insulting her instead.

Back at Hellsing headquarters, Walter reviews the information they were able to gain from "Flesh," as the man in custody calls himself. He refuses to give any additional information, regardless of the incentives offered.

The next evening, Seras investigates the crime scene in plain clothes. She looks around and spots a hidden video camera. Before she can fully investigate, however, two MI-5 agents walk in on her. They identify her as a member of the Hellsing

Organisation and tell her she's out of her jurisdiction. She tries to point out the hidden camera, but they tell her it isn't her job and ask her to leave. Outside, she tries to piece it all together. Arucard talks to her telepathically, saying that she has all the evidence she needs. She begins putting the pieces together.

Meanwhile, back at a computer screen, Kim types in a password while she talks her way through the ethical problem of publicising and filming murder as entertainment. The screen clears, showing footage of two men talking.

Seras is at a bar during this time, spying on Steadler. She orders a tomato juice and watches him, feeling self-conscious. Kim walks in and begins talking to him, and the two leave as Seras pays her bill.

On the tape, the man begins to realise that something's wrong. He thinks he's there for some sort of new drug, but he's very nervous. The other person is a vampire, who begins attacking the man. The video goes dead, the vampire stops feeding, and Arucard drops in. They fight briefly; Arucard makes short work of the vampire. During their battle, an opaque glass wall shatters, revealing Kim and Steadler. They are both nervous and frightened.

Arucard raises his gun, but Seras calls out his name. She is also holding a gun trained on Steadler. She asks Arucard to let human justice deal with the pair, and Steadler agrees cravenly. Seras finds, however, that she would really prefer to kill Steadler after the things he did to her. She is almost ready to do it when Integra and Peter walk in, calming her down and taking Steadler away in handcuffs.

Once Steadler is gone, only Kim, Integra, Seras and Arucard remain. Kim confronts Integra, threatening to show what she has seen to the world. Arucard asks what they should do with her and Integra suggests that Kim should stand trial. On the other hand, she thinks that human law may be insufficient to punish her for her atrocities. Beyond man's judgement and law, Kim is fair game for Arucard. The vampire drinks deeply from the reporter while Integra and Seras watch her death. Seras bites her own arm to hold back her need for blood. Once she returns to the Hellsing mansion, Seras runs into her room, pours the daily package of blood into a bowl and wolfs it down in a frenzy.

ヘルシング部隊
決定稿
UP時
LONG時
階級章

Hellsing

EPISODE: 05

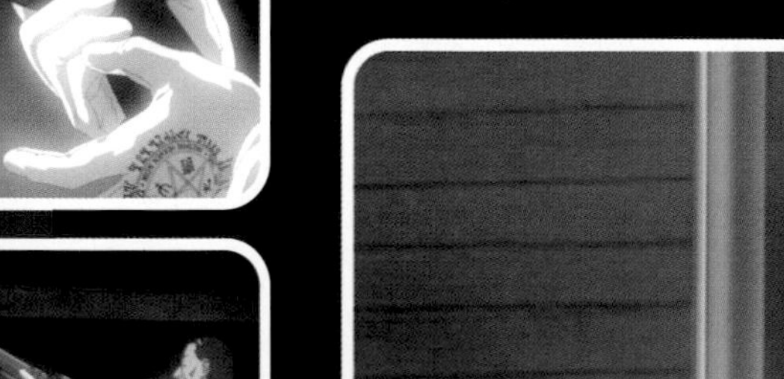

ORDER 05: BROTHERHOOD

The episode opens in a sleazy fetish club somewhere in London. A dumpy man wanders nervously through the club, looking distinctly out of place. He approaches a waitress who directs him to the back of the club. He follows her directions and comes upon a man with long blond hair, wearing a white suit and talking on a cell phone.

As the stranger approaches, he hands the blond man, Luke, a card with an emblem resembling the eye of Horus on it. Luke chuckles and takes the card. With lightning speed, he pulls a gun on the stranger, explaining that the card is a scam. The dumpy man stammers that it's a mistake, that he knows someone named Britz. Luke pauses.

At the Hellsing mansion, Walter places a suitcase on a table. Arucard enters through the wall, and Walter shows him a new black gun. Walter calls it the Jackal and gives its technical specifications. Seras enters the room during this recitation and is confused. Arucard is pleased with the weapon and thanks Walter, who is glad it meets with approval. He also presents Seras with a new weapon, the Halconnen. Seras is a bit nonplussed at the gun, which is bigger than Walter. She doubts her ability to carry and fire it, but both Walter and Arucard reassure her that it is suitable.

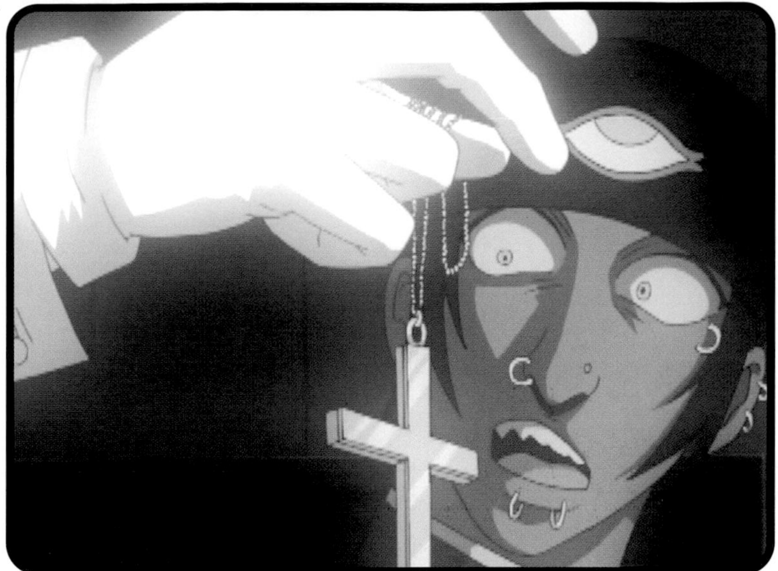

Back at the club, two vampire women feed on the stranger from the first scene while Luke (the owner of the club) and his brother, Jan, watch. Luke states the guy was a cop, revealing a silver cross that the man carried. He tells his brother that he must be from a special ops group that specialises in dealing with undead. Jan recognises the description from Kim's broadcast, and Luke decides that something needs to be done. He crushes the cross and the two begin planning their attack against Hellsing.

The next day, the man from the club is floating in the Thames with the card in his mouth and a British flag planted in his chest. Integra is in Hellsing mansion, telling Walter of the attack. The man in question was an MI-5 agent. Walter is shocked, but Integra quickly moves past his reactions. They agree that a Round Table conference must be called, and begin preparations for it.

Meanwhile, Jan calls into an emergency line, screaming about vampires. He pulls the plug on the phone and sits back with Luke, watching a number of vampiric women feeding on men all around the room. Luke checks his watch and shoots his gun into the air, complaining that they're taking too long.

At the Hellsing compound, the phone call has had a predictable effect. The troops are mobilising and Seras is getting in place with her new gun. Peter and Integra discuss strategy for this encounter, and Integra tells him to be prepared. As the team leaves, Arucard approaches Integra and asks why he isn't going. She tells him that she wants the humans to handle this one, but he disagrees. Nevertheless, he abides by her decision.

At the site, Seras and her unit run inside the building. They find only one ghoul and one vampire, and Seras can tell something's wrong. She is puzzling over this when she realises there's a bomb in the building. Seras throws the soldiers out of the building as the timer counts down. Finally she jumps out the door herself as the bomb explodes, carrying a man with her.

After the smoke clears, Seras slowly digs her way out of the rubble. Peter is relieved, and sends in the report to Integra of the trap and explosion. Integra is angry, to say the least. Once they've returned, Seras tries once again to drink the blood that's been left for her. This scene is juxtaposed with Jan watching a woman dance. He walks over and kisses the girl, then bites her and drinks her blood. Seras, on the other hand, still can't bring herself to drink the packet of blood that was given to her. She puts it away and goes to bed.

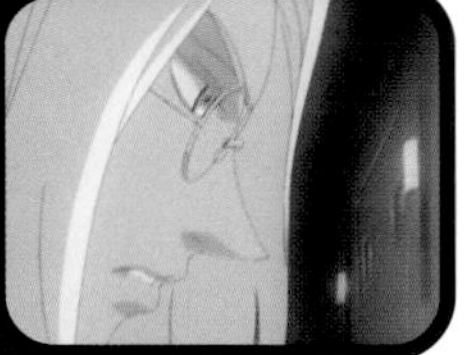

The next day, Integra stands staring at a portrait of her father. A number of older men in expensive sedans are on their way to the house. Walter enters and tells her the knights have arrived and are ready for the conference. She enters the conference room and greets them.

Once the knights of the Round Table are assembled, they begin discussing the Freak chip situation. Accusations and misunderstandings fly thick and fast around the table, with one of the most vocal Knights calling for Integra's resignation on the grounds of incompetence.

The scene changes, following Jan and Luke who are walking outside near dusk. They approach the Hellsing manor house, where a guard stops them. Luke distracts the guard while Jan drives a bus

up to the gate. Around the time the guard gets suspicious, Luke kills him. They then use the bus to ram the gates of Hellsing mansion, breaking down the walls, driving through the front door, and offloading troops. Seras awakes and runs to help as the units try desperately to mobilise.

Luke blows up the Knights' cars while Jan organises the troops. The Knights are terrified, and Integra does a status check with Peter to understand the situation. The troops do their best to hold the invading ghoul army back, but they are unable to halt the ghouls' advances. Unfortunately, the losses that the Hellsing troops have taken are beginning to show, as their own troops begin turning into ghouls and moving against them.

Peter realises that his units are in trouble. From the central command safe room, he calls for help and tries to get the forces to regroup. While he's calling, however, ghouls break down the door. Jan is leading the force into the safe room as ghouls feed on the dead humans nearby. Jan advances on Peter, taunting him with how he will kill him. He laughs as Integra calls over the intercom, trying to get Peter to talk to her. She is interrupted by a shot from over the intercom; shocked and angry, she curses aloud.

Hellsing

EPISODE: 06

ORDER 06: DEAD ZONE

The beginning of this episode is a recap of the last scene from the previous episode, where Jan traps Peter in the safe room. Listening intently to the intercom, the Knights are desperate to know what it was they just heard. Jan uses the intercom to taunt Integra and the other Knights, revealing that he knew that they would be meeting and where.

Seras rescues Peter and removes him from the room. He says he wants to stay there, but she refuses to let him. A few seconds later Jan stands up again, the bullet holes healing. Jan realises that Seras is a vampire and is surprised.

In the conference room, the Knights are frightened. They are anxious to escape, and Integra assures them that they have an emergency escape plan. The Knights want to leave immediately, but she refuses to let them. She notes that the room is armoured, but that nowhere outside this room is as well protected. She is interrupted by an explosion from outside, which she immediately

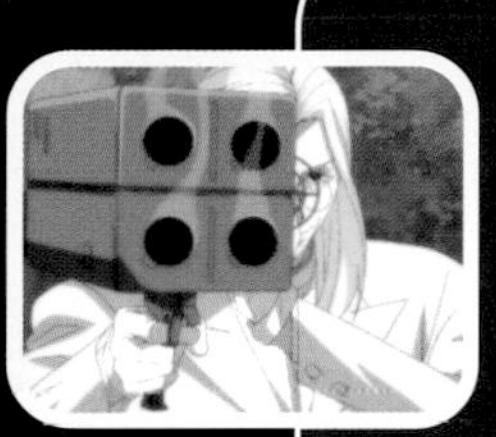

Back in the communications room, Peter is still alive. Jan continues taunting Integra. He finishes his tirade and is ready to finish Peter off when he gets shot in the leg. Surprised, he turns around as Seras fills him with bullets until he falls.

deduces came from the helicopter that was intended for their escape.

Seras carries Peter through the house, until she arrives at her room. Arucard is sitting inside surrounded by dead soldiers. He is mildly surprised to see Peter still alive. Walter enters, still unharmed, and confirms that the first and second floors are lost. They agree that Sir Integra must be rescued, and Walter asks Seras to accompany him up to the third floor. Seras is surprised, but Arucard is amused and pleased to see Walter in action again. Walter asks Seras to bring her new gun along, and though confused, she obeys.

Back on the third floor, the Knights are panicking. Integra tells them not to worry, but they are too frightened to be calm. Finally she loses her calm and tells them off. The Knights are shocked into silence by her outburst.

Jan wanders the halls on the second floor. A nearby door opens and Walter steps out. Walter seems to stand still, but Jan's cigar suddenly falls, cut in half, as does a zombie standing behind him. Walter engages the ghouls and Jan in combat and decimates the front ranks with his monowire gloves, much to Jan's surprise.

Arucard sits in Seras's room, with a bottle of blood and two glasses on the table next to him. He telepathically watches Walter fight the ghouls and laughs to himself. Luke breaks down the door above and enters the room suddenly, but Arucard has been expecting him.

Back on the third floor, Jan calls up more zombies, and Seras takes them out in two shots. Jan takes the opportunity to pull a gun on Walter, but Seras tackles him before he can shoot. Walter's attempts to force Jan to reveal why he attacked them and who he works for fails.

Luke and Arucard begin their confrontation in the meantime. Luke reveals his delight at meeting Arucard and finally having the chance to best him. Luke uses his lightning speed to impress Arucard, and when they finally attack, they both fire their guns and fall.

Jan is still at Walter's mercy, but refuses to speak. His watch timer goes off as footsteps are heard in the distance. Hellsing soldiers reanimated as ghouls under Jan's control attack Walter and Seras. Walter realises that Jan intended to turn the entire Hellsing organisation into his slaves. Seras is shocked, not wanting to kill her own people again and yet realising she must. Jan escapes Seras's grasp and faces off with the pair.

Arucard and Luke recover from their wounds. As they both laugh at the

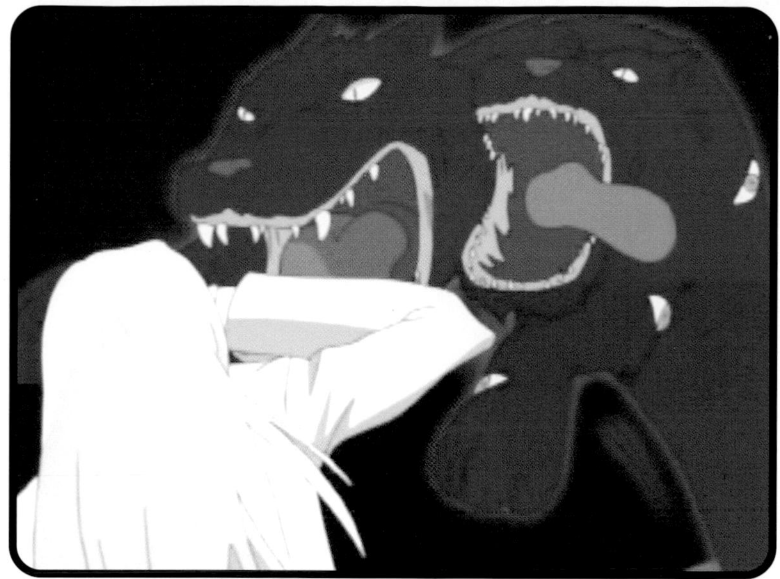

pain, Luke sits up and shoots Arucard again. Arucard fires in return, missing Luke as he uses his super speed to dodge. Luke continues to fight, slowly realising that Arucard shouldn't have been able to recover from the wound he took.

Arucard stands up, smiling. He prepares his magical powers, releasing all his magical restrictions while Luke looks on dumbfounded. Arucard transforms into a demonic black form full of red eyes and fanged mouths. Luke screams in panic while Arucard's disembodied laughter rings throughout the room.

During the battle upstairs, Jan attempts to escape. Walter uses the monowire to catch his arm, but Jan sacrifices his arm in order to flee. Meanwhile, Seras is paralysed with panic and overrun by the ranks of ghouls. The ghouls grab her and hold her helpless as they attack. Just as it seems she might be destroyed, Seras goes berserk and kills all the ghouls nearby. Jan finds his way to the conference room and laughs insanely, aiming his gun at the door and shooting.

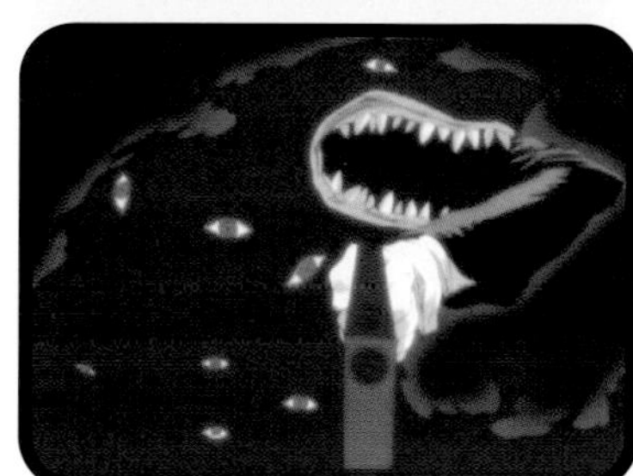

Luke runs from Arucard's demonic form, but is unable to escape. Arucard's gun appears from the midst of the black mass and shoots at Luke, blowing both legs off at the knees. Arucard taunts him to take the fight to the next level, to activate some of the true vampiric powers he claimed to have. When Luke does nothing more than cower, Arucard is disappointed.

Seras continues killing ghouls until there are none left. Walter has to shout her name to bring her back to her senses before she moves on to living targets. Seras is left disoriented and traumatised at what she has done.

In a desperate attempt to save his life, Luke unloads his gun into Arucard. The bullets don't affect Arucard, though. The black demonic form emerges from Arucard's body and heads up the stairs, carrying Luke's screaming body with it.

Jan finally gets the door to the conference room open, where Integra sits with a gun in her hand. She shoots him in the face, then walks into the hall to confront him. Jan laughs, then realises that the bullets are burning. Integra commands him to tell her the name of his master, but Jan sets himself on fire as a last act of defiance. Jan's laughter echoes in the hall as he collapses in a pile of ash, leaving Integra standing in the hall infuriated and alone.

Vampire Myths and Hellsing

In movies, novels, RPGs, and television shows, many myths have become part of vampire lore. Many of them either do not apply to the *Hellsing* series, or are not explored in the first half of the series. Some of the more popular myths are listed below:

1. Vampires sleep in coffins.

This is at least partially true in *Hellsing*. Seras, for example, sleeps in a four poster coffin at the *Hellsing* mansion, and Integra's father tells her that they sleep in coffins during the day. Arucard is never shown sleeping.

2. Crosses and consecrated ground repel vampires.

By themselves, crosses and holy ground do not seem to have much of an effect on vampires. The priest in Episode 1, for example, lives inside a church (with crosses on the walls). Additionally, Arucard is frequently pictured in promotional *Hellsing* material with a cross in his mouth. It seems more telling that all of the blessed weapons are silver of some sort, or are designed for total destruction (such as Seras's Halconnen.)

3. Garlic repels vampires.

This myth is not explored in *Hellsing*.

4. Driving a wooden stake through a vampire's heart will kill it.

Integra's father tells a young Integra that wooden steaks do not work to kill vampires. Nobody tries this during the series, and so viewers can assume that he was correct.

5. Sunlight causes vampires to burst into flame.

Arucard and Walter warn Seras to keep out of daylight, but since Seras does venture outside without much problem, vampires obviously do not burst into flame.

6. Holy water burns vampire flesh.

Holy water is not used in the series.

7. Vampires do not cast reflections.

No vampires in Hellsing are seen close enough to a mirror to test this myth. Arucard uses a mirror to watch over young Integra in *Order 10: Master of Monster*, but it doesn't truly show his reflection in that scene.

8. Pure silver damages vampires.

Silver and silver bullets are more typically associated with werewolves rather than vampires. In *Hellsing*, though, silver is the ammunition of choice against the undead since it greatly damages vampires and ghouls. In one of the final scenes, Arucard uses molten silver from a large cross to kill Incognito.

9. Vampires possess the power of flight.

Vampires are never shown flying in *Hellsing*, although some can levitate.

10. Vampires prey on virginal Women.

In *Hellsing*, vampires prey on everyone.

11. Vampires turn into bats, wolves, and/or green mist.

Both Arucard and Paul Wilson turn into beasts during the series. These creatures are far more terrifying than normal animals.

12. Vampires drink blood to survive.

This popular myth is retained in the series.

13. Vampires live in Transylvania.

Arucard's origins are not revealed, but he currently lives in London, England. Incognito is likely from somewhere in Africa.

Hellsing

Episode: 07

Order 07: Duel

Duel opens with a funeral, on a rainy British day. With Integra, Walter, Seras, and other soldiers looking on, the slain are laid to rest. As the mourners disperse, Integra flashes back to the aftermath of the battle at the Hellsing mansion, where she was forced to shoot some of her own men to prevent them becoming ghouls. Back in the present, she says that for her, there is no forgiveness, and that the situation is all her fault.

At the ruined Hellsing headquarters, Walter recounts the results of the attack: 135 dead, 57 survivors, 24 of those wounded. Fargason has a broken jaw, but will return to duty in two day's time.

Somewhere else in the city, Seras — in street clothes, psuedo-undercover — enters combat with a ghoul in an alleyway. From a building in the alley, someone watches her through the shutters on his window. She slays the ghoul, then is told via radio to proceed to Hyde Park for a rendezvous.

Back at Hellsing HQ, Integra and Walter plan co-ordinated research on the Valentine brothers and their background, with MI-5, in the name of revenge. The Knights of the Round Table have asked that MI5 assist with the investigation. Integra says that this is about vengeance, and those responsible for the attack and Freak chips will pay a thousand-fold. A wax-sealed envelope from The Iscariot Organisation arrives, with an invitation to visit the National

Galleries. Although she appears angry at the invitation, she attends anyway.

At the National Gallery, Enrico Maxwell, head of The Iscariot Organisation, and his assistant, Father Renaldo, approach her. Integra refuses to shake his hand. Enrico offers his condolences and sympathy over the recent attack, but Integra does not want to hear it; she is still upset over Sir Paladin Alexander murdering Gareth Henderson, and tells Enrico that he should leave the country. He tells her to shut up and pay attention, then reveals details about the Freak Chips. He calls it a "bug problem" — indicating that they are originating in England — and declares that The Iscariot Organisation will not hesitate to wipe Hellsing off of the planet if they cannot contain the chipped vampires. As Enrico insults Integra — calling her a "squealing English sow" — Arucard appears behind Integra. He says that the Romans haven't changed in over 2000 years — they still think the world belongs to them.

Elsewhere, Hellsing forces are fighting a large number of ghouls. Seras, underground, relays the details of a target on the train to the commander, who relays them to Walter. Walter deals with the transit authority to quickly close the stations and stop the train, preventing the target from endangering more human lives. Immediately afterwards, evidence of Sir Paladin Alexander's presence in London — in the form of images showing his blessed papers pierced by swords — is shown to Walter, who commands his secretary to alert the National Gallery and call a "Code 00767."

Arucard says he doesn't believe that he can allow Enrico to leave alive. On a train car in the London Underground, Sir Paladin Alexander slays several ghouls with his swords while moving from car to car. As Arucard is about to pull the trigger on one of the men in the museum, a voice comes over Enrico's radio. Even with the speaker using code names (Captain Hook for Sir Paladin Alexander, Tiger Lily for Seras, The Lost Boys for the other Hellsing soldiers) it's clear that Sir Paladin Alexander is ready to kill Seras. Integra storms off, while Arucard trades more verbal barbs with Enrico before leaving.

On the trains, Seras finds the dead ghouls and the telltale purifying wards of Alexander. At the gallery, Arucard (Peter Pan, according to the code names) says that he will take the fight to Alexander, and leaves. Alexander handily kills several Hellsing soldiers as they ineffectually shoot at him. One of his swords slashes Seras's rifle, and she looks at it in shock until Arucard shows up. Arucard and Paladin Alexander duel on the train, with Alexander restraining

Arucard with his scrolls, then slicing a train car in half — and severing Arucard's head from his body. He throws the head to Seras and drives one of his swords into it. Seras then fires her pistol at him repeatedly until throwing herself out of the train window to avoid another sword. She lands in a heap on the tracks while still holding Arucard's severed head.

Seras begins to walk away from the scene of the fight, holding Arucard's severed head and wondering aloud what she should be doing. In the train car, Arucard's body slowly melts, becoming a red mass with many eyes, which then morphs into a cloud of bats. As Alexander closes in on Seras, the swarm surrounds and distracts him. Arucard's head turns into a pile of insects, Seras screams and drops them, and they coalesce with the bats to reform his full body, head attached. Paladin Alexander calls Arucard a monster, and Arucard says that must make Alexander a man, a dog, or another monster.

They duel again, Arucard firing twice at Alexander and blowing off both his arms. Knocked to the ground, Alexander flashes back to a previous time — perhaps his first meeting with Arucard. In this meeting, Arucard stands over Paladin and appears to use mind control to force him to turn his gun towards himself. In the real world, left with few options, Alexander desperately picks up a sword between his teeth and runs towards Arucard, who at the last minute shoots the sword, breaking it to pieces. They stand face to face, and Alexander claims that the next time they meet he will kill Alucard — the "black magician of Hellsing" — and then the Paladin disappears in a stream of blessed papers.

Arucard turns to Seras, telling her that Alexander has no chance; he is neither man nor monster, and only a man can truly kill a monster.

At a restaurant in the museum, Enrico and Renaldo walk in as Integra walks out. She pauses, saying that Hellsing will not yield and The Iscariot Organisation should run from them. As she walks outside, she notes what a beautiful day it is.

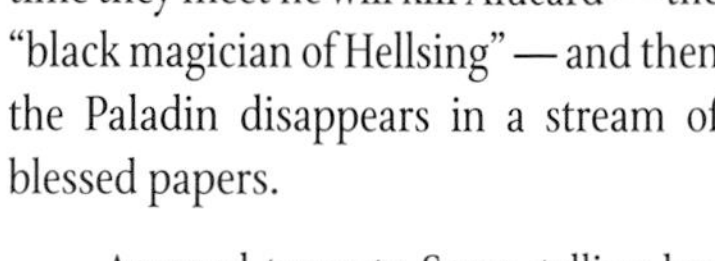

Hellsing

Episode: 08

Order 08: Kill House

This episode opens in Hong Kong with a team of Hong Kong police operatives raiding a Freak chip manufacturing operation on the fourth story of a warehouse. One of the people working the Freak chip operation shoots one of their own men to stop him being interrogated, and a firefight ensues. Some of the operatives are injured, but one of them throws a grenade, destroying part of the building and all of the evidence.

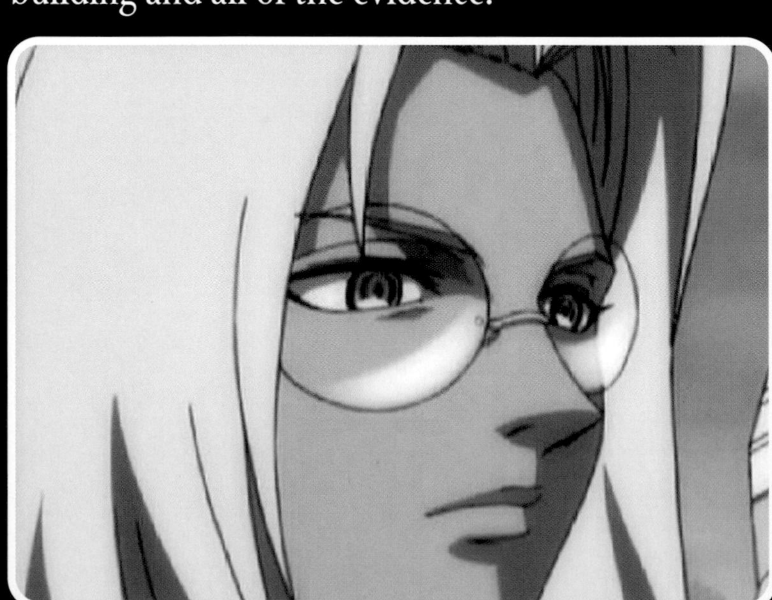

At a secure training facility nea Stonehenge, Integra and Fargason watcl new recruits train in a speciall constructed maze, complete with decoy and live fire. Walter expresses hi displeasure at many of the new recruits beliefs — heathens and atheists — bu understands that in times like this they need all the support they can muster Seras instructs a group of rag-tag potential soldiers on how to act and where to shoot during the maze tests until one of the applicants says that he heard there is a "rea mpire" in the unit. The group laug Seras steps up and bends the barrel of his MP5 informing him that he better have i replaced or else he'll miss the chance to take the test.

In a Palo Alto, US desert, a car ha swerved off of the road and flipped onto its side. A police helicopter identifies the dead driver as a suspect in some unnamed crime.

A presentation on the Freak Chip takes place amongst members of the Knights of the Round Table. They believe the chips combine semiconductors and biotechnology, but they still can't figure out how the Freak chip goes from there to vampire — it may act on something in latent DNA. This theory is not proven, though, and there are other theories about the Freak chips, not explained at this time. Integra claims that a Freak is a Freak, and Hellsing opposes all of them — and Hellsing will search and destroy! Integra believes that the Freak chip creators are human, because they are reacting in relatively predictable human-like ways to prevent Hellsing and other authorities from gaining more information about their operations.

For the first time in what appears to be weeks if not months, Seras returns to her London apartment. She spends her time preparing some food and looking at pictures of her father, in his police uniform, and her as a child. She apologises to her father, since she can no longer eat the real food that they used to share when she was young, and says that she feels so wrong; finally being a police officer but being so different from him. The wind picks up, and she goes to close the window. Just then, there is a knock on the door. Nervously, Seras turns off the lights and draws her gun before asking who is outside. When she opens the door, the man there is Harry Anders, one of the MI-5 agents last seen in *Order 04: Innocent as a Human*. She invites him in for tea, and they begin to talk. He eats the food that Seras had prepared, and says that she must know that this meeting did not happen. Harry claims that he used to know Seras's father, but before he tells her about it they need to go somewhere together.

Harry drives Seras to what looks like an apartment building, where they take the elevator to the roof. Harry knocks on a mysteriously large door located on the roof, introducing himself and asking to come in and speak to someone named Helana. Inside, a single room that looks like a large library is lit only with candles. Opera music plays in the background. Helena speaks softly, and when she stands she is very short, barely four-feet tall. She inquires as to how Seras became a vampire, but Seras does not answer. In turn, Seras asks her how long she has been a vampire. Helena says that it has been far too long. It is perhaps here when Seras realises just how immortal vampires truly are, as Helena still appears childlike, though she does not speak like one. Helena turns to Harry, asking why she is being harassed, for she does no harm to anyone.

Harry briefly explains the new Freak chip vampires, before mentioning that Seras belongs to Hellsing. Seras quickly says that she only kills — no, "disposes" — Freak chip vampires, not natural ones. Helena places her hands on Seras's chest and concentrates, as if reading her mind or browsing her memories. She learns that Arucard also belongs to Hellsing, and that he is Seras's master. Helena tells Seras that she is blessed. Harry asks for information about Helena and her "cabal", of which Helena denies the existence, saying that they are all individuals, free from petty forms of human bondage. While she is immortal, she still has much that she wants to do, and does not wish to be disturbed. She says that no English vampire was involved in the construction of Freak chips, but to build a replica, an original is required. She then bids the visitors good night.

Harry and Seras have a brief discussion on the way back to her apartment about drinking blood; Seras says she only drinks transfusion blood. Harry begins saying "Christ, if I was twenty years younger...." It's unclear whether he was implying that he would like to be a vampire, or if he was proposing a tryst with Seras. After dropping her off, Harry's car suddenly explodes while driving away, likely killing Harry instantly.

Under some sort of mind control or illusion, Integra imagines being tied to a pole inside the training facility's maze when a group of trainees come through the door, weapons at ready. A new character is seen standing on top of a hill, long jacket blowing in the wind. Glowing red symbols like those on Alucard's gloves (see page 48) appear in the sky as Arucard releases Control Level Restriction Two. The maze crumbles around Integra and she falls back to the physical plane, as the symbols fade in the sky.

Alucard appears, asking Integra if she knows what it feels like to be hunted. He says that he has always been pitted against pretenders and frauds, but now a worthy enemy has come from the continent, and that he can't wait to duel with them. Wind sweeps over the hills, and the new vampire — tall, with white skin, facial piercings, a bald head and long coat — is on a hill above them. His eyes glow bright red as the episode ends.

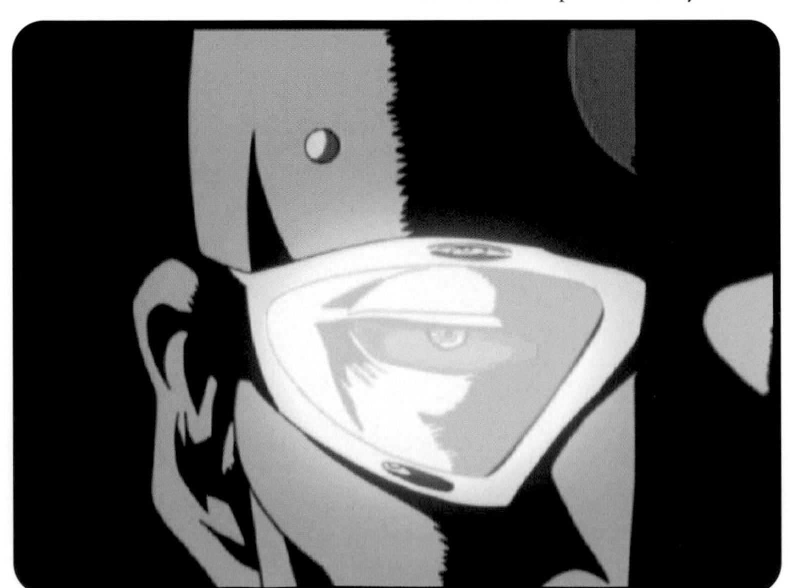

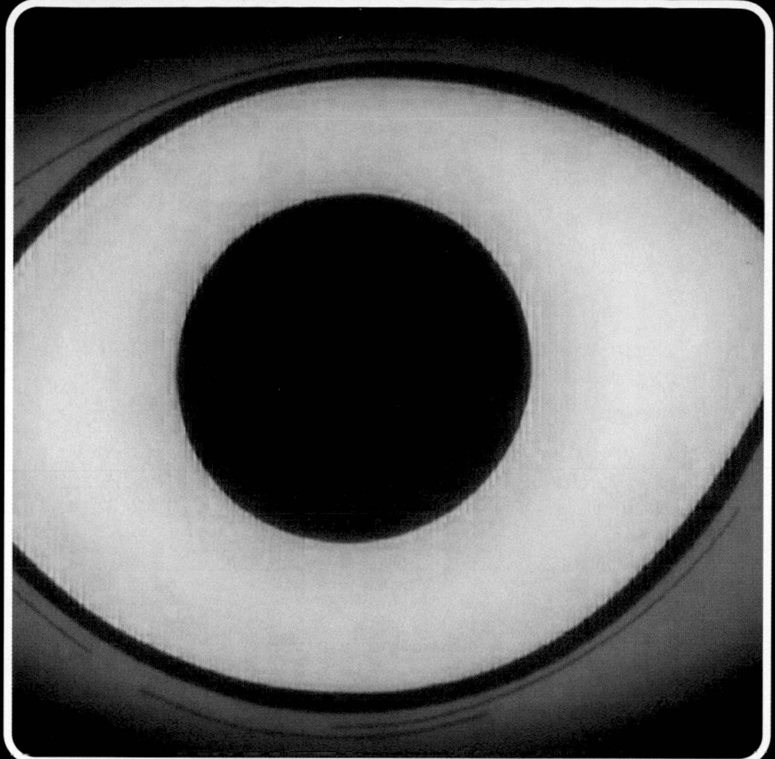

ORDER 09: RED ROSE VERTIGO

Integra sits in a helicopter, surveying the scene of Bobhan Castle. The castle is owned by a Japanese company, but is currently on the auction block. Hellsing plans on raiding it that night, since they suspect it is home to Freak chip vampires. As Integra's helicopter lands, the new vampire watches her from somewhere unseen.

The raid on the castle is set to begin, with Hellsing forces on land and in the air at ready. The front door is kicked in and just inside the soldiers see a body, lying as if crucified, on large flight of stairs. A single gunshot is heard. At the top of the stairs stands a shadowy figure, unmoving. Seras pauses, expressing concern about the situation but not explaining exactly why. Sergeant Pickman listens briefly on his headset radio, and then calls for a retreat. Even though she was hesitant to go in, Seras looks confused as to why they are withdrawing.

As Hellsing withdraws, over a dozen helicopters — some transporting armoured vehicles — arrive on the scene. They are SAS vehicles, and a man disembarks from one of the helicopters and orders Hellsing to withdraw. The SAS agent claims that the castle is a known hideout for IRA members, and thus it is the SAS's responsibility ... even if the members are no longer human. After being chastised by the agent,

Integra orders a complete Hellsing withdraw. Hellsing officers begin leaving the castle, leaving Seras alone inside. Arucard speaks to her via telepathy, telling her that she must be prepared for what is to come.

At the Hellsing mansion, Walter welcomes Integra back, and mentions that a Miss Laura is waiting for her. Upstairs, Integra greets her "dear sister" while looking dazed. Sitting down, Integra cuts open an envelope while admonishing Laura for showing up without warning. Laura says that the Avon family is doing well, and Integra appears to fight back either tears, or a sudden headache. Integra offers Laura a guest room for the night, which she accepts.

In bed at Hellsing HQ, Seras senses something strange and wanders upstairs, where again she sees the same image of a body lying on a stairwell. A black cat walks across the room, startling her. Seras stares at Laura as she moves about upstairs, until Walter interrupts her from behind, startling her again. Seras asks about the woman and Walter explains that she is Integra's little sister. Suddenly, Walter looks pained and grabs his chest. After a few moments he regains his composure, but excuses himself immediately afterwards so he can get some rest. Seras looks around again, believing that something strange is going on.

In the middle of the night at Bobhan Castle, an SAS soldier inside an armoured transport vehicle drinks from a cup of coffee. Bored, he begins to tell a ghost story — about Nazis and demons in Transylvania during World War II — to his partner, who does not respond. Finally he spins his partner's chair around, revealing the sunken eyes and slack jaw of a new ghoul.

On a table in a large room bathed in blue light, drops of blood dot a thin man's body. His eyes are open, but he appears unaware of his surroundings. He has a conversation with a disembodied voice, the voice offering him the ability to live forever and be a perfect being. In the end, the man says he wants to live forever, and Freak chips crawl out of a blue liquid below the table, implanting themselves in his body.

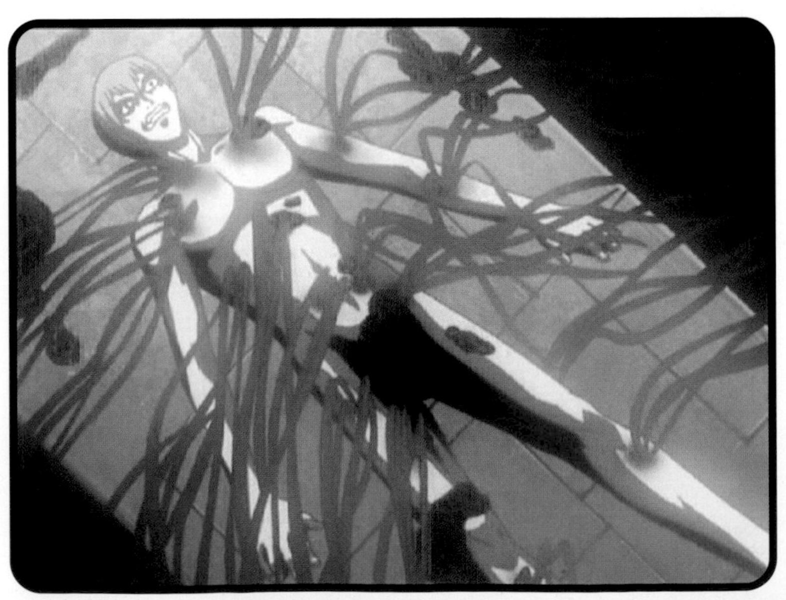

Asleep at her desk, Integra has a very confusing dream. In it, images of herself as a baby flash by, then a scene from a church, of a skeletal man that appears to be the grim reaper floats towards the ceiling, carrying a woman. The woman wears a pink dress and has long blonde pigtails down to her ankles. Next the dream flashes to a dead person in a bathtub, and finally to the shadows of a prison door closing.

Arucard is in Bobhan Castle, calling out the new vampire and asking for his name. Arucard says that this new vampire is pitiful for also having a human master.

In the Hellsing mansion, Laura wakes up Integra, who is dazed. Seras tries to run upstairs, but is blocked by Walter — obviously under someone's influence — who tells her that she is not allowed to disturb Integra. Walter then cuts Seras across the cheek with his Monowire Garotte.

Laura undresses Integra, removing her jacket and shirt, leaving her in a plain white undershirt. Integra appears unable to move, but can still talk. She says she doesn't have and never had a sister. Laura ignores her and leans down, biting Integra's breast through her shirt.

In the castle, the unknown vampire steps out, saying that his name is "Incognito." Arucard mocks him, saying that Incognito is nobody ... but his own name is a bit of an enigma, too. Arucard further says that they are both originals bound by humans, and, while pulling his gun, that they should both have some fun.

Laura continues to lick Integra's breasts while Integra questions her, asking her if the Hellsing Organisation destroyed her people. Integra says that Laura is petty for coming to settle such an old score, and that she's not even worth Hellsing's soldiers time. Frustrated, Laura stabs Integra in the stomach with Integra's own letter opener. Downstairs, Seras yells at Walter, telling him to wake up. Integra begins to bleed from the mouth, and Laura mocks her, telling her that she has a dirty mouth.

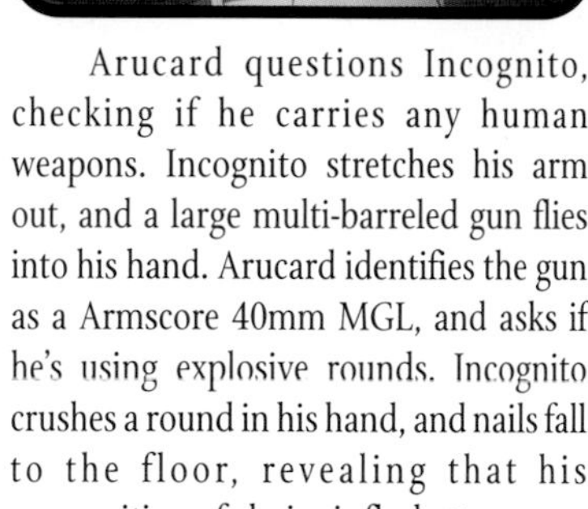

Arucard questions Incognito, checking if he carries any human weapons. Incognito stretches his arm out, and a large multi-barreled gun flies into his hand. Arucard identifies the gun as a Armscore 40mm MGL, and asks if he's using explosive rounds. Incognito crushes a round in his hand, and nails fall to the floor, revealing that his ammunition of choice is flechettes.

Meanwhile, Walter has tied Seras up with his monowire, preventing her from moving at all. Laura licks up Integra's blood, telling her in detail about how she was supposed to delay the process, but now she's going to make her into a mindless ghoul. As she bites into Integra's neck, Arucard's symbols appear in the night sky above the Hellsing mansion, and he appears. Walter breaks free of whatever was controlling his mind and rushes upstairs with Seras.

Arucard confronts Laura (known as "Boobhanshee"), who screeches and launches herself across the room at him. He disposes of her with a single silver bullet. With Arucard, Seras, and Walter looking on, Integra cuts her own neck open to free herself of the impure blood in her veins.

Hellsing

Episode: 10

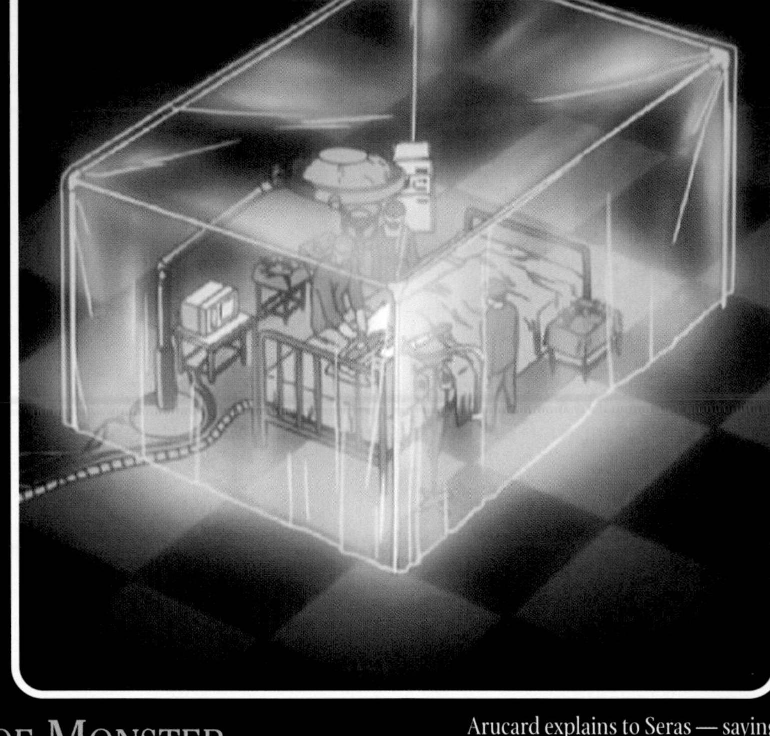

Order 10: Master of Monster

In a makeshift hospital room in the Hellsing mansion, doctors tend to Integra. Arucard and Seras stand watching as Integra lies motionless, hooked up to a respirator and being fed intravenously. Seras apologises, blaming the attack on herself and saying she should have been able to stop it.

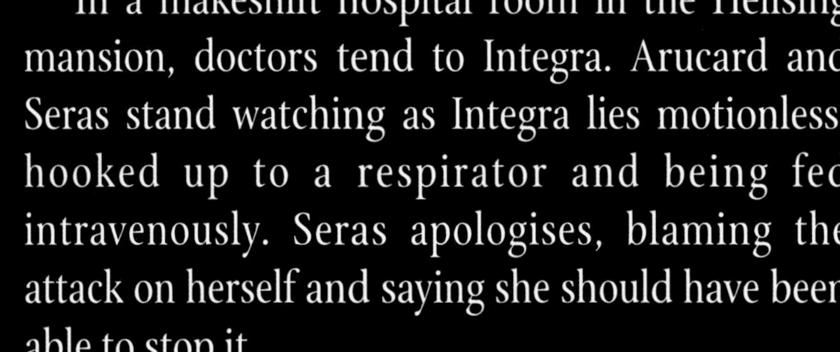

Arucard explains to Seras — saying that she must listen carefully — tha Integra refused to give up, going so far as to tear out her own throat to save herself Arucard tells Seras that by doing so Integra has gained true strength. The doctors begin surgery on Integra.

Walter speaks with someone over the telephone. Bobhan castle has been destroyed, and the 66 members of the SAS squadron are missing.

As the surgery continues, Seras looks increasingly uncomfortable before walking out without a word.

During the surgery, Integra flashes back to her childhood, probably in her early teens. Waking up late, she goes into her father's office. As she leaves he room, a swirling pattern and eyes appea on her bedside mirror. In his office Integra's father and her talk abou vampires, as he dispels some of the

childish myths about them (wooden stakes will not kill a vampire). He continues to talk about Hellsing's mission to serve Britain and how they proudly carry the proverbial "Holy Shield and Righteous Sword." As they talk, his hands appear to age suddenly, and he passes out.

Later, in his bed, Integra's father speaks to his brother Richard, his daughter Integra, and family butler, Walter. He asks Integra to lead the family and the Hellsing Organisation, and for Richard to be her guide. As he takes his last breaths, he tells his daughter to always "Be Glorious."

The scene briefly flashes back to the surgery continuing in the real world then back to Integra's dream, where she is crawling in a passageway above one of the floors in her house. Back to reality, where Seras sits alone on the steps to Hellsing Mansion, the shadow of a cross cast over her body in the fading daylight. Asleep, Integra cries, as does young Integra in her dream.

Crawling in the passageway, young Integra hears voices, and crawls close to a grate to get a better look. Looking down into an office, she sees Richard and four other men. Richard tells the men to search everywhere for Integra — he has waited 20 years to take control of the Hellsing Organisation, and does not want to give it up to a brat. He thinks that Integra is hiding in some of the lower locked-off levels of the Hellsing house, and orders the men to find and kill her. As Integra curses her Uncle for being heartless, she remembers something her father once told her: "If you should ever be confronted with true crisis, where all hope is lost, make your way to the forgotten underground prison. There, in one of the cells, lies your salvation."

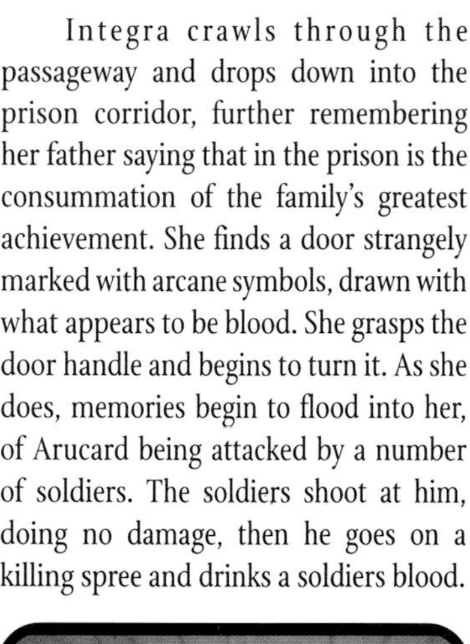

Integra crawls through the passageway and drops down into the prison corridor, further remembering her father saying that in the prison is the consummation of the family's greatest achievement. She finds a door strangely marked with arcane symbols, drawn with what appears to be blood. She grasps the door handle and begins to turn it. As she does, memories begin to flood into her, of Arucard being attacked by a number of soldiers. The soldiers shoot at him, doing no damage, then he goes on a killing spree and drinks a soldiers blood.

Richard and his four guards arrive in the prison, pulling guns on Integra as she stands with her back to the door. He threatens her, sending a warning shot just to the side of her face and then presses the muzzle of the gun to her, saying he has no problem killing a young girl. Integra gathers her courage and opens the door, diving through it and down a small stairwell.

Away from the dream sequence, Walter is setting up tea for Integra when Seras walks by. He apologises for his actions the previous night, even though he did not commit them wilfully. Seras is surprised that he is making tea for Integra when she's still in surgery, but Walter talks about General Patton and how his attention to his soldiers in battle would inspire them, implying that Integra would do the same for the Hellsing Organisation.

Back in Integra's dream sequence, Richard shoots her as she falls into the prison cell, spilling blood across the floor. The men and her both catch sight of a humanoid being, tied securely to the wall. Neither Integra nor Richard has seen it before, and they have no idea what it is. In the confusion, the figure leans down and begins to lick some of Integra's blood from the floor. After drinking the blood, he breaks free of his bonds and attacks the men, ripping one of their heads clean from his body. Integra reacts with fear and revulsion, realising that this man is a vampire and that her father had something to do with him.

Integra grabs a gun and points it at the man's head, but he only laughs and says that he has finally tasted blood for the first time in twenty years. Integra shoots him several times with her pistol, then verbally lashes out at him, saying that she is Lord and Master of the Hellsing family and would die before allowing a vampire to order her. The vampire laughs, not feeling threatened by the girl or her gun. Integra says again that she would die before giving up, as it is her duty and pride as leader of the Hellsing Organisation. The man says that she makes his blood boil, kneels at her feet, and dubs her "Sir Hellsing," then calls her "Master."

While they are distracted with each other, Richard — one arm torn completely from his body earlier in the scuffle — fires his pistol at Integra. The man rises and dives towards the bullet, blocking it with his arm inches before it would hit her. Integra rests her gun over the man's arm, pointing the pistol at Richard.

In the present, Integra and Arucard have a short telepathic conversation about how Arucard will always think of Integra as that little girl, and then Integra wakes up.

Incognito is shown on a tiny island. He has his large gun strapped to his back, and is sitting around a small fire. Performing some sort of ritual, he summons great waves of water which freeze as they rise into the air. The man roars again and the ice shatters, revealing that each one held a trapped SAS soldier-turned-ghoul.

ORDER 11: TRANSCEND FORCE

Seras is in what appears to be a prison cell, sitting on the floor. A ghostly image of Paul Wilson (first seen in Order 09 becoming a Freak chip vampire) appears, floating in the air. He's carrying a woman, and leans down to bite her throat. When she bleeds, blood flows across the floor from between the stones in the wall. Paul tells Seras that they are one and the same.

Seras wakes up, whimpering for Arucard. Looking around the mansion, she finds him with a wheelchair-bound Integra on the balcony, looking at the night sky.

In London, a car with official flags drives around. As it passes near a bridge, the bridge is hit by a rocket and collapses. Back at the Hellsing mansion, Walter and Integra discuss recent news of an attack at a girl's dormitory in Cambridge. Some of the victims were mutilated, while others drained of blood; the distinction was made on whether the girls had a sexual history or not. The attackers appeared to be about 60 ghouls, roughly the same number of men who disappeared from the SAS unit. Walter looks at pictures of the SAS unit members, one of them being Paul Wilson. In addition, the previous attack at Trafalgar's Square was done with SAS issued equipment. Walter lets Integra know that a Round Table conference has been scheduled, but due to her condition she is not expected to attend. She says

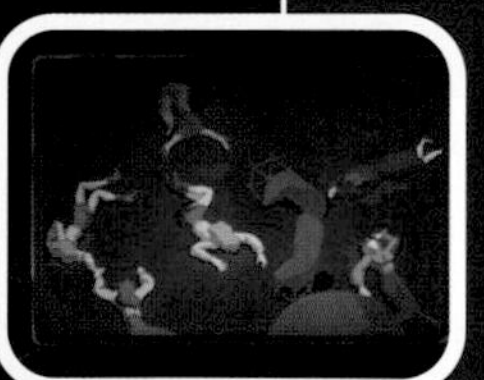

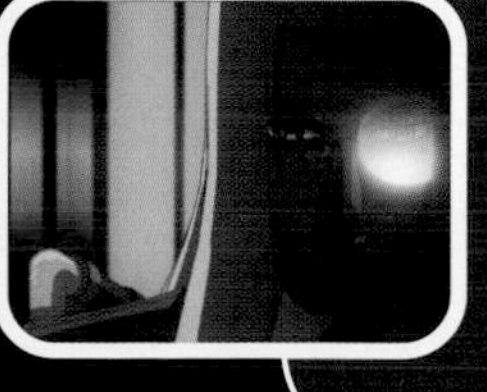

there is no need for a conference, and that Her Majesty already has a plan.

A white car shows up at the Hellsing mansion. Two men enter the mansion while Seras looks on. After they are out of sight, Seras notices Paul standing by the side of the road. He flickers and disappears as Peter Fargason comes up behind her. Asking Seras if she's alright, he then directs her to stand at attention, and dismisses her from the Hellsing First Action Unit. He reassigns her to Hellsing Information Retrieval. He explains that the changes are necessary because her presence seems to affect the morale of the new recruits, but that she is still a member of Hellsing and needs to show her pride.

Further newscasts state that Buckingham Palace and Scotland Yard is on alert, believing that the terrorists are still in London.

The two men from the white car leave the mansion and drive away. In Integra's office, a burned note is seen in her ashtray. She stands, saying "her royal order" under her breath, and goes to Arucard's room. Arucard says that humans are amusing, and asks Integra if she's ever thought about asking him to have her drink his blood. She asks why he hasn't read her mind, and he says he wants to hear her say it herself. He knows that she's stronger than many humans, but the upcoming enemy is like no other.

Integra interrupts; the Queen has given her an order for the first time. Arucard seems impressed, remembering the first time the same thing happened to her father. As Integra leaves, Arucard once again asks her if she wants to drink his blood. She pauses briefly, then continues walking.

London is heavily guarded, police everywhere. SAS soldiers-turned-ghouls storm through the sewers. A news bulletin says that the Queen is going to the Tower of London under heavy security. Integra tells Walter that the Queen is actually coming to the Hellsing mansion for a ceremony.

Seras, in street clothes, knocks on the door to Helena's rooftop flat. Sounding upset, she says she needs someone to talk to, but nobody answers. She kicks the door down, finding the room empty. The needle on a nearby record player skips.

Reporting to Integra, Peter Fargarson says there has been a Freak attack at the Tower of London. Integra sends her Hellsing soldiers to deal with it, leaving her home defenses in the hands of the Secret Service.

In Helena's house, Incognito steps out of the shadows, telling Seras that she is powerless. His mouth is covered in blood, and he drops a blood-covered

shoe. Seras fires her pistol at him, but he quickly regenerates, pushing the bullets from his body; they fall to the ground like teardrops. Incognito asks Seras if she regrets not drinking blood to get stronger, or perhaps she regrets letting Arucard drink her blood in the first place. Something else stirs in the apartment; the record player is knocked back to it's starting position and begins to play, and the pages of some books blow about in an unseen wind. Above, the sky glows red through the window. A ghostly Helena appears behind Inognito, then disappears. Incognito spins around, firing a couple rounds randomly. One of them knocks over a candle, which falls next to a bookshelf.

Seras and Incognito look around, when a hand begins to push it's way out of Incognito's stomach, followed by the imprint of Helena's face as she begins to push her head and shoulders out of his body. Incognito pulls out a knife and raises it above his head. Seras screams, and he backhands her with his gun, leaving her stunned. With his other hand he brings the knife down, cutting Helena's head off. The head falls to the floor, and Incognito walks off.

The sun sets and the moon rises. Seras is left crying in Helena's apartment. Her disembodied head speaks, explaining to Seras that when an immortal body and soul is torn apart, their essence is allowed to wander the heavens. She tells her to be a worthy and loyal companion to Arucard, and they must destroy the evil from the dark continent. Finally, she warns that Seras's companions are about to fall into a very

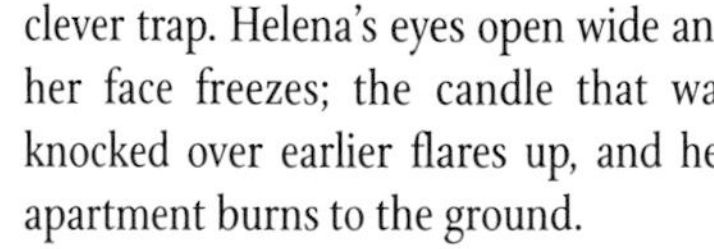

clever trap. Helena's eyes open wide and her face freezes; the candle that was knocked over earlier flares up, and her apartment burns to the ground.

News reports begin to come in about armed police forcing their way into the Tower of London. Fargason talks to the other commander, explaining that they will be combating SAS soldiers implanted with Freak chips, so they must all shoot for the head or neck. Meanwhile, Seras races down the street, yelling into her radio, trying to get in touch with the others from Hellsing. More news reports filter in, this one about bombs and gunfire inside the tower.

In the Hellsing mansion basement, Arucard's runes appear, and he tells Integra that the Queen is not coming, and Integra is to stay at the mansion while he leaves to "have fun."

Further news reports indicate that the terrorist organisation attacking London is named Hellsing.

Hellsing

Episode: 12

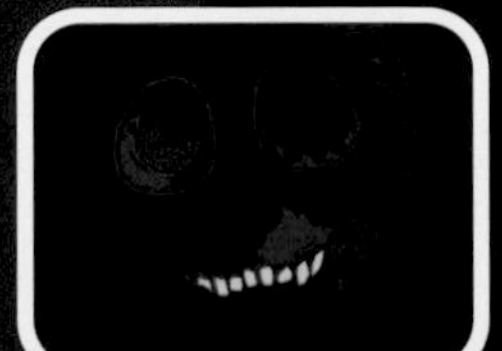

Order 12: Totally Destruction

This episode opens with flashbacks from and expansions upon *Order 11: Transcend Forces.* Hellsing's Gamble Squad is attempting to surround the enemy in one of the towers. The former SAS agents turned ghouls attack them from behind. Meanwhile, Seras runs towards London Tower, trying to reach anyone from Hellsing to inform them of the trap.

Peter Fargason commands one of the units over the radio to backup Gamble Squad, but gets no answer. As he steps out of his vehicle, British military vehicles ram it, while other units surround him.

It is revealed in a conversation between Walter and Integra that there was a traitor in the Round Table meeting: the British Army was given permission to attack Hellsing.

Elsewhere, Hellsing's Pickman Squad fights their way through crowds of ghouls towards Beauchamp Tower. The group is ambushed, and just as things look especially dire, Arucard arrives, saving the remaining soldiers. They share a quick word about their losses to date, and how they cannot go home without a victory. This is one of the few times that Arucard speaks to anyone who is not Seras, Integra, or Walter.

Sir Integra phones the Knights of the Round Table and verbally lashes into

them, upset that they are trying to take her family's honour. Walter then phones Fargason, but he doesn't answer.

Peter didn't answer the phone because he's been pinned down by a line of soldiers. Seras begins to run towards him, but he quietly tells her to stay away. From a hotel room across the street, a sniper targets Peter.

Integra nearly collapses onto her desk, sweating profusely. Walter tries to tell her that she must work within her limits.

Peter tells the soldiers to stand down, and that he will not let the British Military impede Hellsing's investigation. A news helicopter flies overhead, shining a spotlight down at him. Peter fires his pistol once, into the ground, and the British soldiers kneel down just before the sniper shoots Peter twice; once in the head, once in the heart — right through his Hellsing patch. In her office, Integra's eyes open wide as she appears to sense Peter's death.

Seras runs towards Peter's body, telling the soldiers to stand down. They obey, and she hugs the body, gently licking some of the blood from around his mouth. She then runs into one of the armoured vehicles, and emerges moments later wearing her usual blue uniform and carrying the Halconnen. As she tries to leave, one of the soldiers calls her a traitor. She fires the cannon above the soldier's heads, and then runs toward the towers.

An overhead shot reveals that the Hellsing mansion is surrounded by police cars. The news radio reports Peter Fargason's death, listing his military achievements. Around town, civilians watch the news, cursing Hellsing and Fargason. Walter pledges his life to Integra, and she says she will never surrender, but will not resist now. She thinks there is still hope for Hellsing and their forces.

Seras fights her way to the tower, taking out ghouls with her pistol on the way. She finds Arucard inside the tower, and he tells her to enjoy herself. Near the tower they find Pickman; he begs them, saying that he wishes to die human, for Hellsing. Arucard grants his wish, shooting him and then laying his hat over Pickman's head. While Seras stays outside, Arucard goes to the base of the tower and calls out for Incognito.

Paul Wilson appears outside, attacking and tackling Seras. Pinned to the ground, she spits in his face while he mocks her, saying that she is no better than a ghoul. He says that she should discover a new life ... with him. She headbutts him, knocking him off of her.

The two men first seen in *Order 11: Transcend Force* return to the Hellsing mansion, bringing a message from the Queen to Integra. The message says: "These are times that test the heart, Sir Integra Wingates Hellsing. The Royal Family will not forget the contributions of the Hellsing Family over this century. Please stand strong through this fierce night and take solace that at sunrise your judas shall be punished. Remember that your majesty's prayers are with you." Integra takes this to mean that the Royal Family has abandoned Hellsing. The power at the mansion flickers out.

Confronting Incognito on the top of one of the towers, Arucard releases "Control Art Restriction Level Two, Situation B, keeping restriction unlocked until target is eternally silenced." At the same time, Incognito's purple runes glow across his body. Outside, the man fighting with Seras transforms into a werewolf.

On the roof of the Hellsing mansion, Integra and Walter prepare to fly away in a helicopter. Walter handily cuts apart the police officers' guns, rendering them useless before he takes off, piloting the helicopter for the first time in years. Integra is short with Walter when he says he may not quite remember how to pilot the craft as well as he used to.

Arucard and Incognito prepare to duel. Arucard is still overjoyed that he has an opponent that he believes is worthy of his time. Meanwhile, Seras continues her fight with the werewolf, knocking it to the ground and shoving a Halconnen shell into its mouth. The shell detonates and his blood showers her just after she tells the beast to go to hell and beg for His forgiveness on the way.

Early in the duel, Arucard believes that he has won. He asks Incognito who his master is, and who is making the Freak chips, but Incognito just laughs. Purple runes like the ones that sometimes appear on his body begin appearing on the walls and ceiling of the room they are in. At a crucial moment, Arucard has no silver bullets remaining. Incognito's eyes glow purple, and he blasts Arucard with laser beams, cutting him up. Just then, Seras runs in with extra silver bullets. For the second time in a short while, Seras is told to run away, but before she can, Incognito turns his laser beams on her, cutting through her neck.

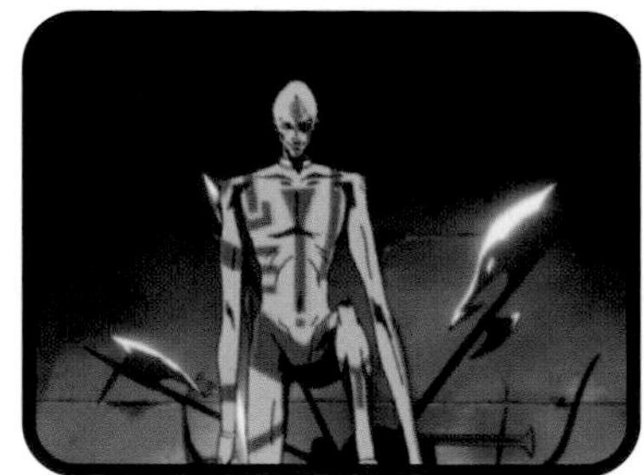

The episode closes with a news report announcing that the Royal Family is safe, and that London's own special units are going to clean out the tower.

Hellsing

EPISODE: 13

Order 13: Hellfire

On top of one of the Towers of London, the bleeding Seras reaches for her gun. As Arucard and Incognito argue, Seras's spare clip flies into Arucard's gun and Arucard fires at Incognito from close range, blowing Incognito's head clear off.

Purple rune lines appear across Incognito's body, and his head reappears. He pulls a metal piece from his face and flings it at Arucard's gun, magically infusing the shards so they shatter the barrel. This in turn sends fragments of Arucard's silver bullets up into his face, and Arucard's body melts into a pool of sticky blood, his head still resting on top.

In the helicopter, Integra urges Walter to move faster. British helicopters pursue, commanding them over the radio to turn around and follow their instructions. Walter ignores them and turns the radio off. Walter says that he wishes that they had installed Sidewinder missiles, and Integra stoically says they'll talk about it at the next budget meeting.

Seras crawls across the floor towards Arucard. He sadly tells her that she should have listened to his advice, and his head begins to sink down into the bloody mess. She wraps her arms around his head and softly licks up some of his blood. Again, he tells her to run. Incognito jams an axe into the ground near Seras, telling her that she will never be a true nosferatu, and that she has nothing to be afraid of because she's already dead.

One of the British helicopters fires on the Hellsing helicopter. In the

combat, the side window and part of the passenger door is blown off, and Integra falls from the helicopter. Walter rushes to the open door, and uses his monowire to catch Integra as she falls, carefully looping it around her blanket. Holding her up cuts his hands, yet he manages to drop her to the ground from only a few feet in the air. The British helicopters fire again, and this time the Hellsing helicopter crashes to the ground behind a building, with Walter still inside.

The next scene shows Incognito and Integra inside one of the towers; Integra has been pinned to the ground by four spears. Incognito is in the middle of some sort of summoning ritual, and there is a large silver cross in the room. Integra asks him what he's summoning, and he replies "Rott Gar! Sett!"

Outside of the tower, a beam of blue light bursts out of the ground, and arcs towards a group of British soldiers. It hits them and bounces off the ground, starting a swath of destruction through London. Incognito tells Integra that he is going to bring Sett into his body so he is even more powerful, and that he will also take her.

Integra calls out Situation A, to release Control Arts Restriction Level One, Cromwell Initiative. She further yells "your master Hellsing commands it!" Incognito leans down and bites her on the throat, but she barely reacts. When Arucard does not appear, she screams for him. The blue light of Sett continues it's path of devastation through London, then Incognito raises both his arms into the air and screams.

One of the dead soldiers from Order 12 is shown, blood flowing away from his body. Blood flows from Seras's body in the same manner. Arucard's voice is heard announcing the release of Control Arts Restriction Level One, and his red runes appear on the ground, covering all of London and about half of the Southern UK. The area directly around London Tower glows bright red, and a multi-eyed dog runs towards the towers.

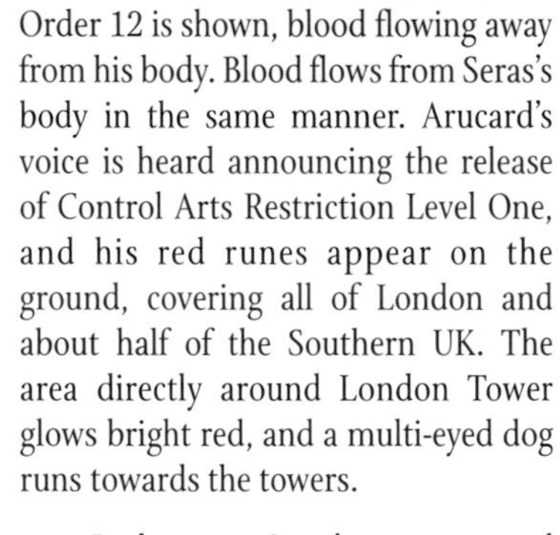

In the tower, Seras's eyes open, and Arucard stands over her. He still doesn't have his hat back, having left it on Pickman. His hair is longer, nearly to the floor. He says that it's a beautiful night, and then disappears, reappearing in the same room as Incognito and Integra. He explains that he revived himself by feasting on the blood of the tower.

Incognito turns himself into a beam of blue light with a snake's head, and launches himself into the air. Walter is seen being wheeled away on a stretcher. Incognito flies down to attack Arucard, yet Arucard manages to hold him off by holding his jaws open. Incognito says that Arucard will become a part of him and serve Sett for eternity!

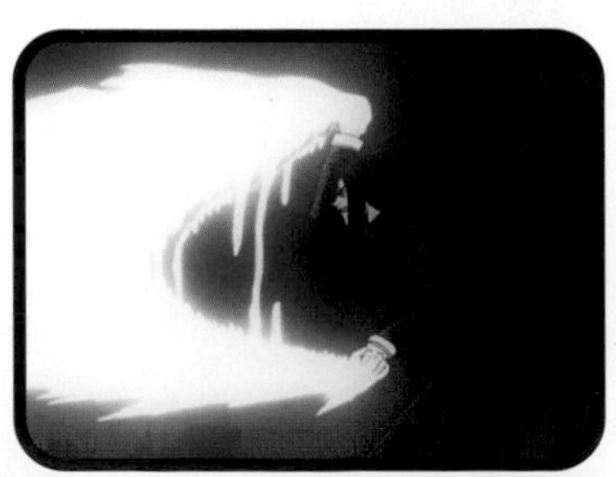

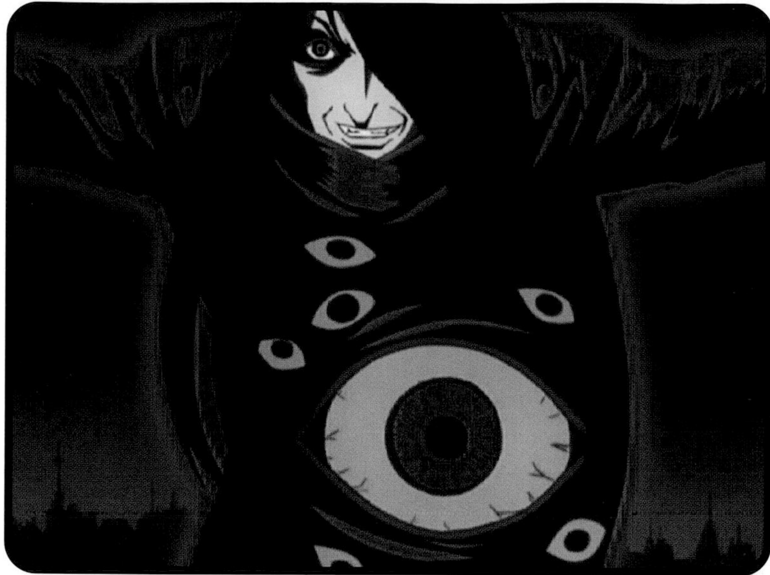

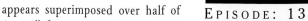

A big eye and multiple small ones appear on Arucard's chest, and two large beasts begin to grow out of his body. They are each over 4 metres tall and have the head of a giant wolf.

Incognito suddenly turns into a sound wave, sending a thin beam outwards at a great speed; the beam cuts through Arucard and many of the surrounding buildings. On the ground, Sir Paladin Andersong watches the destruction unfold.

Arucard's wolf-heads fight with the blue light snake in the sky, defeating it and sending it crashing from the sky through one of the tower buildings. Outside of the tower, Seras tends to the weak and wounded Integra.

In humanoid form, Incognito tells Arucard that he has been imbued with the power of ancient gods, and he welcomes eternal pain. Arucard says that he will give him exactly that! They duel again, with Incognito peppering Arucard with flechettes. Arucard fires his broken gun at close range, somehow blowing a hole in both himself and Incognito. Arucard uses his powers to

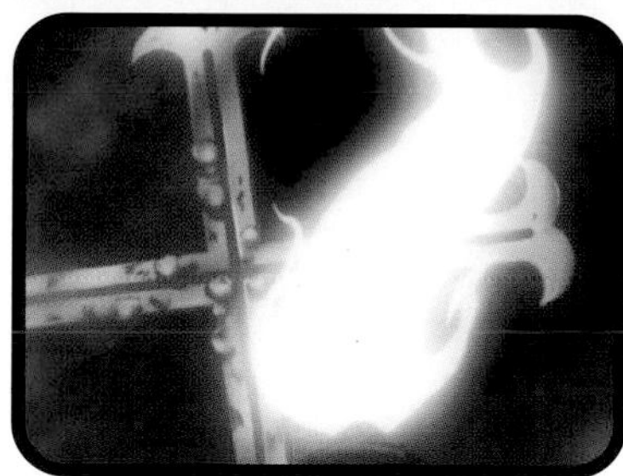

begin melting the silver cross; the molten silver flows down, into Arucard's broken gun. Incognito mocks him for trying to use a broken gun, but Arucard plays the trump card, sending the liquid silver straight towards Incognito. It hardens quickly, and Incognito is impaled on a long silver spike.

Incognito asks Arucard who he is, and an image of someone who appears to be the legendary Vlad the Impaler appears superimposed over half of Arucard's face.

Incognito is shown impaled on a spike again, this time attached to the tower vertically. Incognito is displayed for all to see, his gun still hanging over his shoulder. Over a blank screen, a text message says that the traitor in the Round Table was discovered and brought to justice, and that MI-5 is still investigating the Freak chip vampires.

In the Hellsing mansion prisons, Arucard and Integra are inside a locked cell; two guards are posted outside. Integra's wrists are cuffed together with leather handcuffs. Arucard asks her for his orders, then shatters a blood-filled wine glass in his gloved hand. He offers the dripping blood to her, and she smiles slightly. The episode ends without a resolution to the question: does Integra taste his blood or not?

Arucard's Gloves

In an interesting artistic choice, all the main characters in *Hellsing* wear white gloves on their hands. There appears to be no particular reason other than as an anachronistic fashion statement, a nod to *Dracula*'s Victorian setting, or an understated clue to the viewer as to the importance of a specific character. Arucard's gloves, however, may be an exception to this.

On the back of each of Arucard's gloves is what appears to be an arcane symbol. It consists of a five-pointed pentagram inscribed inside a circle, with strange astrological or alchemical characters in the spaces between each of the points.

There is a band of writing around the outside of the circle with the following inscription: "Hellsing • Hells Gate Arrested • Gott Mit Uns • And Shine Heaven Now." Gott Mit Uns is intended to be "God with us" or "God be with us" in German. Outside that band are more unusual characters, written in a strange runic script. Using letter substitution, it becomes clear that the runic words are English, writing out "Hellsing," "Hells Gate Arrested," and "Shine Heaven Now." At the bottom of the circle, toward the wrist, is a square with rounded corners and four horizontal lines, making a ladder of sorts within the square.

The importance of the symbol is not made clear within the series. It may be a magical symbol that has something to do with his agreement or bond to the Hellsing Organization. It may simply be his way of announcing his affiliation with the group, much like the badges that the uniformed soldiers wear. It might also be a clue as to the reasons behind his continued affiliation with Hellsing and Integra: a hope of salvation for his soul.

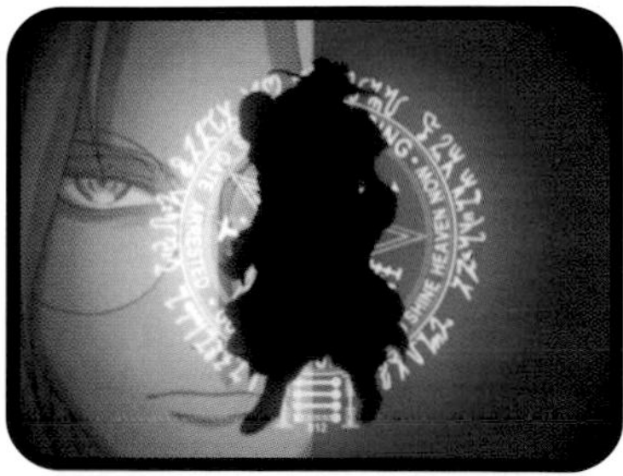

HELLSING CHARACTERS

Hellsing is a series about the supernatural, a tale of horror set around the idea that men's ambitions and dreams can be more dangerous than the worst monsters our age-old fears could dream up. When faced with a theme such as this, many horror stories focus on the human element, the interaction between characters, to keep the audience from losing touch with the moral of the story. By placing ordinary people in a moment of surpassing terror and forcing them to rely on one another to survive, the fundamentally good portions of their character are revealed. The audience is left at the end with a sense that regardless of the evils in the world, the good in human nature can always find a way to pull through.

Not in *Hellsing*.

In *Hellsing*, the monsters — utterly inhuman monsters — are the good guys and the main protagonists. The good humans are just the supporting players, working behind the scenes, while the bad humans are the villains, transforming themselves beyond the bounds of Nature. They use science to do things Man Was Not Meant To Know in order to achieve their dreams of power. There are no deep-seated friendships here, no willing martyrs for the good of their fellow man. Not even Seras, who wanted unlife for the straightforward reason of avoiding the finality of death.

As a result, there is very little in-depth character interaction in *Hellsing*, certainly not to the extent other series show. Just finding some friendly camaraderie can be a stretch. In the first six episodes, only Seras really evinces any character growth, and that's not much. Everyone else has been living among the evils of hell for years, and they're quite used to the neighbourhood. Some of them even rather like it. There is no need for heroic histrionics here.

Hellsing instead uses that very inhumanity to highlight the absence of redeeming human values. By personifying the struggle in Seras and keeping the redeeming, empathic good values confined to her, the series is able to underline the horror of its premise without focusing on messy interpersonal details.

ARUCARD

Arucard is a mysterious figure. A supernatural vampire of untold age and power, he acts as the Hellsing Organisation's secret weapon. His reasons for doing so, however, as well as his true motivations, remain unknown.

Arucard's first meeting with a young Integra Wingates Hellsing comes when he saves Integra from her Uncle Richard Hellsing, who attempted to take over the Hellsing family business following the death of Integra's father. Imprisoned in the lower level of the Hellsing family mansion — unknown to everyone except Sir Hellsing — for over twenty years, Arucard is freed when he tastes the blood of the teenaged girl. Integra impresses Arucard with her commanding attitude and sense of purpose. It is at this point where Arucard dubs her "Sir Hellsing."

Arucard's name, of course, is the most obvious hint to his origins — "Dracula" spelled in reverse, with an "r" replacing the "l". This would seem to indicate a tie to the old Dracula story of the 1800s, especially given his tie to the Hellsing Organisation (in Stoker's novel, Dracula's nemesis was Dr. Abraham Van Helsing).

Arucard's powers include the abilities to walk through walls, cling to surfaces, become invisible, teleport over large and small distances, regenerate wounds, transform into insect swarms, transform into a formless demonic creature, transform into a wolf-beast, telepathy, flight, opening portals to hellish dimensions, regenerate after being "killed", mind control, complex illusions and other powers that have not yet come to light. In addition to what has been shown thus far, he has mentioned the ability to change into a bat or fog and summon demonic servants. It is assured that the limits of his powers have thus far not been tested.

His position within the Hellsing Organisation is one of unique status. He is the agency's ace in the hole, answerable only to the Organisation's chairman, Sir Integra Hellsing. To the majority of the world, he remains completely invisible. Only a few other top-level personnel in related agencies know of him, and those are mostly other knights of the Round Table. Those who do know of him typically refer to Arucard with fear and loathing, holding him up as a mark of shame against the Hellsing Organisation for fraternising with the creatures they are sworn to destroy. His abilities, however, are one of the key assets that keep the Hellsing Organisation with acceptable personnel losses.

Within the organisation, Arucard answers only to Integra. He accepts assignments from her, reports to her following each mission and even, on rare occasions, seeks out her company for conversation. Their relationship has obviously lasted for years, but it has never become casual. This is due in part, no doubt, to the subtle reminders in every conversation that, while Integra is the one giving orders,

Arucard is a creature of vast power who obeys only because he chooses to do so. Were it not for his undefined agreement with the Organisation, she could never control him. Still, the power of her position is never in doubt, and this unspoken agreement is what allows them to work together smoothly.

Outside of Integra, Arucard's only other contacts are Walter and Seras. Whereas Integra is obviously Arucard's superior (if in name only), Walter is a comrade. He has fought with Arucard for years, rising far above the rank and file in both ability and understanding. He now serves as Integra's assistant, responsible for Arucard's daily needs. In that way, Arucard relies on Walter, forging a closer and friendlier bond than any other characters in the series share. Arucard also shares some discussions with Sergeant Pickman, and Arucard kills him to prevent him from becoming a ghoul — at Pickman's request.

On the other side of the coin is Seras, or as Arucard calls her in his mocking fashion, "Police Girl." Seras is still a young woman in many ways, unable to cope with the harsh realities of the world she has been thrust into. His appreciation of her bravery in the face of terror was likely what induced him to make the offer of unlife to

her in the first place. By doing so, however, he placed himself in the unlikely position of being parent and master to a fledging vampire, one who was utterly unprepared for what her new life would require. Though he can see that she has potential, she has a long way to go before achieving it. Arucard does not understand her reservations and has little patience for them. He has been inhuman for too long to commiserate with her difficulties, if he ever suffered them in the first place. She does, however, help alleviate his feelings of endless boredom.

Arucard's outlook on life is difficult to understand. He seems to revel in the role he plays in the Organisation, seeking out rogue undead and disposing of them. This seems odd, and most of the vampires he fights and destroys find it utterly beyond their understanding. One interpretation is the idea that a) Arucard is very old, b) he is very intelligent, and thus c) he is very bored.

Arucard is a predator. It is the nature of a vampire, as Seras continues to discover. He is not simply a predatory monster, though. He is a thinking creature, with a mind finer than that possessed by many men. He is witty, self-possessed, and even charming in a frightening sort of way. Add to that centuries of preying upon humans who don't even possess the tools to truly challenge him, and it adds up to boredom. He even admits it straightforwardly in Episode 5, when asking Integra to let him go with the troops to try out his new gun.

This may be the reason that he hunts other vampires. It gives him a chance to hunt prey that might pose a challenge to

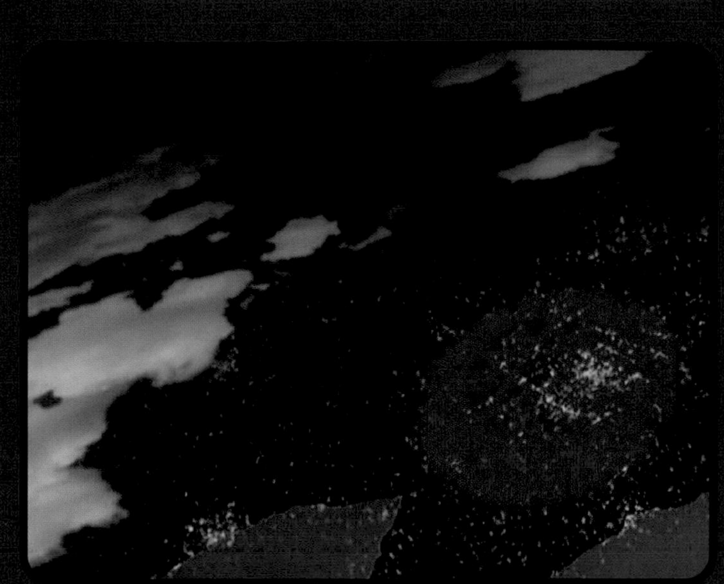

him, however small. He probably uses guns for similar reasons; they force him to rely on his mind rather than his supernatural powers. They also limit the chance of witnesses (should there be any) becoming aware of his vampiric nature. It may play very heavily into his embrace of Seras, simply to find a companion in his deathless existence, one whom he could teach and mould into a suitable partner.

An interpretation is that Arucard is filled with rage; an anger against fate and his lot in life. He typically allows that anger to surface only when he hunts, resulting in the scathing diatribes he uses as he taunts his prey. The source of this hostility is uncertain, but the two most likely causes are his vampiric nature and a sense of rage at the part fate has forced him to play.

Arucard's nature as a predator means that he is cold, cruel, and calculating. If these traits were not part of his personality in his mortal life, it is certain that centuries of vampiric existence has impressed them upon him. Additionally, his inescapable boredom and the agreements binding him to the Hellsing Organisation force him to keep much of his natural tendencies bottled up with no outlet.

He does not hunt human prey, instead allowing Walter to provide him with nourishment in the form of blood collected at a medical facility. A very tame method of hunting, to be sure. He does not roam the night, instead spending much of his time at Hellsing mansion when not on assignment. In short, he does none of the things that vampires typically do, instead reserving all his abilities for the needs of the Hellsing Organisation.

It is obvious that Arucard finds a sort of irony in this arrangement. His sarcastic humour is always in evidence with both Seras and Integra. He delights in causing discomfort, reminding them of the inhuman monster he is. In reality, he may be far more human than either of them realise or are willing to accept — something that doubtless amuses him even more.

Through the series, Arucard undergoes some striking physical changes. When he is imprisoned in the Hellsing Mansion, his hair is long and pure white, and he's wearing a complex straightjacket and plain black gloves. When he returns from near death in Order 13: Hellfire he has longer black hair and a red version of the straightjacket with white gloves. The most interesting physical change happens in the final episode. In the climatic moment of Incognito's sudden death, lightning flashes over Arcuard and an image of a slightly different face is superimposed over his. The new face appears only briefly, and Incognito is shocked by this final revelation. The most obvious and telling feature of the new (or, rather, old) face is the long thick moustache, and the wild eyes. The alternate identity appears to be Vlad Tepes — better known as Vlad the Impaler, or the original Dracula. For more information on this possible link between Arucard and Dracula, see page 79.

SIR INTEGRA WINGATES HELLSING

Though never directly stated, Integra is probably the descendant of Dr. Abraham Van Helsing (or Hellsing, as the name is spelled in this series). She is the head of the Hellsing Organisation, a group devoted to the destruction of all undead within Britain. She is also a member of the Knights of the Round Table — a group consisting of the leaders of the British government's highest security ministries that is devoted to the safety of the nation. She resides at Hellsing mansion along with some other members of the Hellsing Organisation, who reside in buildings somewhere on the estate. Her age is uncertain, but likely falls somewhere in her late-twenties or early-thirties.

The only relative of Integra's that is mentioned in the series is her father, and he died sometime prior to the time of the series. Her mother died when Integra was young — perhaps while giving birth, as a strange dream of Integra's seems to allude to. Integra was an only child, despite the illusion-laden murder attempt by the vampire Boobhanshee, who posed as her nonexistant sister. The only other family member is her Uncle Richard, who was killed when he tried to wrest control of the family from Integra after her father died. She remains devoted to the memory of her father, as indicated by the portrait of him hanging in her office and the time she spends looking at it when she needs to think. She does not allow that devotion to handicap her when it comes to determining the best course of action, though. She may have adored her father, but she does not intend to make over herself or the Organisation in his image.

It seems that the Hellsing Organisation is a family affair, and the running of the organisation would have been more likely to be given to a male who could be certain of carrying on the name, if there were one available. That would also explain her habit of wearing men's clothing, as a way of attempting to compensate for being born the "wrong" sex.

Integra is a cool customer. Her work, her image, the Hellsing Organisation, and her family's legacy are all deadly serious business to her, with no room for levity or error. She is brusque with nearly everyone, Walter being the exception. She rarely smiles and never jokes, though a dry sardonic sense of humour does make its way to the surface occasionally — usually in a macabre fashion that gives those around her pause. She is highly intelligent but rarely shows the workings of her mind to anyone.

In addition to her previously mentioned mental attributes, Integra has one more quality that keeps her on the edge of her game; she actually likes her job. More than that, it might be even fair to say that she loves it. She is a crack shot, the equal to anyone in her employ, and she practices regularly even though there is little chance she'll need to use her skill. She has a keen predatory instinct, and can appreciate the skill and grace of the hunter in all its forms, even when arrayed against her. She is well acquainted with the darker side of the world, and finds herself at home and comfortable with it. She devotes her every waking moment to defending Queen and Country against the forces of hell, but her fervour in responding to threats is that of a she-wolf defending its territory, not a patriot serving her nation. She is undoubtedly the best-qualified person in the world for her position, and she knows it.

There are only two people in the series presented as possible equals to Integra. The first is Arucard. While theirs could hardly be described seriously as a relationship between equals, her status does counteract his supernatural power to an extent. They are evenly matched as far as intelligence goes, and they both have a

grudging respect for one another; a respect that is a key component of the basis of their relationship.

Arucard serves as an irritant to Integra at the same time, due to his refusal to keep to his place and his ever-present reminders of his powerful and inhuman nature. She does her best to both overlook what he is and use it as a tool against him, to keep him at a distance. She hides her feelings for her subordinates, not wanting to show any weakness. Too much emotion would immediately sabotage her hold over them.

Walter is the second individual who breaks through the icy reserve she uses with subordinates. Since Walter is a retainer to the Hellsing family, it is likely that she has known him since she was a child. He is certainly nearly old enough to be her father, having long since retired from active service in the Hellsing Organisation and moved on to butler, bodyguard, and right-hand man. Integra never forgets that Walter is her servant and employee, but she allows him to hear her thoughts, feelings, and suspicions in a way that no one else does. It is obvious she trusts him implicitly, and equally obvious that trust, with Integra, is never blind.

As for Seras, Integra has neither the time nor the inclination to bother herself with a "half-starved vampire who can't even protect her commander." She does not understand why Arucard embraced the girl, and she's more than a little put out to have to provide for someone who can't pull

their own weight. It is clear from the other Round Table members' comments in Order 6 that she takes quite a bit of heat for having Arucard around from those who don't understand their arrangement. To bring another vampire home will undoubtedly make her life that much more difficult. If Integra has any motherly instincts, she keeps them packed away in the attic.

Integra's status among the other Round Table members is competitive, to say the least. Integra is a vital member of the organisation, as indicated by the proceedings during the meeting with the other Knights. As in all political groups, however, there are always people vying to take her position away. The Knights of the Round Table betrayal of the Hellsing Organisation deals a serious blow to Integra. While she is used to having her work cut out for her, this turn of events occurs at the worst possible time. Obviously, the Judas had been waiting for his opportunity to strike at Hellsing. She is left angry and dismayed; not only has her family's honour been tarnished, perhaps permanently, but some of Hellsing's best men were lost in the battle at London Tower.

Integra does not seem inordinately religious, although if anyone has proof of the existence of life beyond death, it's the Hellsing Organisation. The cross she wears is as much a symbol of her Organisation as it is a belief in a higher power. Still, she seems to hold no animosity to the half-pledge, half-prayer offered before her troops exterminate a vampire, and her statements of "May God and Her Majesty be with you," are never facetious. She is, very aware of the division between Catholic and Protestant, and guards the dividing line between them much as the angels guard the gates of Eden, bearing a sword of undying flame to keep the Vatican — and the Iscariot Organisation — at bay.

At the end of the series, Arucard offers his blood to Integra. While she does not drink, her actions both then and previously (in *Order 11: Transcend Force*) indicate that she at least contemplates it. While it may seem strange that the Hellsing Organisation's leader would wish to become the thing they hunt, there are several compelling reasons for her to do so. First is the extra amount of power it would grant her. She would become a fierce hunter and warrior in addition to her already keen managerial and directorial skills. Second is the immortality, which would enable Integra to maintain control of Hellsing for an indefinite amount of time. This is vitally necessary in the coming years, since her human mortally combined with lack of heirs — Integra has no siblings, no children, and no procreation partner — will catch up with her and the Hellsing Family legacy eventually. Whether she could simply have a relationship with Arucard and bear his child is not even suggested, and there appear to be no other suitable partners for her.

Seras Victoria

Seras Victoria (her last name is Victoria, not her first) is a young woman in her early twenties. She was originally an officer in the London Police Authority. She was promoted into the D-11 elite squad, a unit assigned to handle unusual, sensitive, or especially dangerous situations, often working in conjunction with other government agencies.

A short time after arriving in D-11, Seras's unit was assigned to a situation in the village of Cheddar, where most of her unit was killed. Arucard, a vampire in the service of the Hellsing Organisation, embraced her during a mission. Following her rebirth as a vampire, she was transferred to the Hellsing Organisation where she is attempting to fit in and learn the rules of the new harsh world in which she now finds herself.

Seras's original job profile was never explained. When she first appears, she is wearing a SWAT-style field uniform and carrying a gun, assigned to find and apprehend a priest believed involved in the disappearance of several individuals. Her natural aptitude, however, seems to be in the area of investigations. Certainly her sensitive and emotional nature seem ill-suited to infantry-style combat, so perhaps her position in D-11 was as a specialist of some sort.

While in D-11, Seras had a close relationship with the other team members, almost as a type of mascot. Her youth, rookie status, and cute appearance undoubtedly determined her relationship with the team. The members of the team nicknamed her "Kitten," and she was on a first-name basis with all of them. Peter Fargason at Hellsing claims that they treated her with kid gloves, shielding her from the worst of the experiences. He is likely right, given how unprepared she was for shooting a human, or even someone who simply appeared human.

Seras was very fond of the D-11 members, and seems to look on them almost as her family. She still keeps a group picture of them and finds herself looking at it often. To have them killed by a vampire and turned into ghouls was especially traumatising for her, and an event that haunts her to this day.

During her assignment in Cheddar, Seras made her biggest decision to date: to cheat death and accept Arucard's offer of unlife. Whether she knew entirely what she was getting herself into is another question entirely, but regardless, she met her fate with courage and resolve. She was willing to be killed in order to prevent the escape of a monster, and to return from death in order to keep that same monster from winning. In the end, what she didn't count on was becoming a monster herself.

Seras is a very confused, conflicted individual. Possessed of a sensitive nature in a profession that demands a tough exterior, her young life would be difficult even without the added problem of becoming a vampire. No family members are mentioned, so it is unlikely that she has any currently living relatives with whom she can communicate and share the trials of her new life. It is even more unlikely if she did have any that the Hellsing Organisation would allow her to contact them anyway.

Without any form of emotional support, Seras is ill equipped to handle the changes in her life. While she accepted Arucard's offer unflinchingly, she never dreamed of the changes it would bring about. Perhaps it is too much to expect that she could have, knowing nothing of vampires or the supernatural before her harrowing experience in Cheddar. She finds her new vampiric nature to be a horrifying thing. She cannot accept that she is not now, and never will be again, human — a price she would not have willingly paid if she had only known beforehand.

Seras fights endlessly against the demands of her new existence, clinging to her humanity with every bit of will she has. She will not drink blood, her only sustenance, until driven to it by the demands of a weakened and starving body. She is hurt by the unwillingness of others to enter into a friendly relationship with her. She rejects her predatory instincts, giving in only when overcome by her need to survive and left traumatised by the results.

Cast adrift in all areas of her life at once, Seras's relationships with the others in Hellsing are both confusing and infuriating. She has no one with whom there is common ground. The other soldiers set her apart because of her vampiric nature, but among the inner Hellsing circle, she is sometimes ignored and treated in a condescending manner because of her youth and inexperience. Still, there are seeds of hope that Seras can find her place with assistance from Peter, Walter, and Arucard.

Peter Fargason is the head of military operations for the Hellsing Organisation, and is primarily in charge of Seras's training in the field. He chooses her assignments and oversees her progress, along with occasional suggestions from Sir Integra. While Peter is unsparingly blunt regarding Seras's performance, he also offers her much needed encouragement. Under his tutelage, she is learning to become a better officer and an efficient field operative. Peter is tasked with removing Seras from the Hellsing First Action unit late in the series after several events show that she is hurting the morale of the team. She returns to unathorised active duty after the death of Peter Fargason during the London Tower raid.

The next important individual in Seras's life is Walter. Walter was assigned to Seras soon after her arrival at Hellsing mansion to see to her daily needs. He provides her with sustenance (when she'll partake of it) and ensures that she is provided with any other needs she may have. He is also one of the only individuals in Hellsing mansion who treats Seras with respect — something she needs more than she realises.

Part of Walter's respectful attitude toward Seras is simply his proper British retainer persona. He calls her "Miss Seras" and takes all her comments very seriously, something no one else does. Walter's relationship with Seras is not close or intimate, but there is the possibility of him playing a fatherly role toward her. He seems to genuinely care how she is feeling or what she does, and that appearance is enough to keep her going for now.

Finally, there is Arucard, Seras's vampiric "father" and master. For reasons known only to himself, he offered her the gift/curse of vampirism and now must train her to use her new powers. If Seras was hoping for a deep empathic relationship with Arucard, however, she was sadly mistaken.

Arucard is hardly perfect himself, but Seras's stubborn inability to accept her new life has him stumped. He does not understand her misgivings, her fear of her new inhuman nature. He wants what is best for her, but he has no tender emotions or fatherly concern to give to help her come to terms with it. Instead he gently mocks her, eavesdrops on her thoughts, and generally plays the stern taskmaster. On the occasions when he does try to help her more directly, such as offering her a way out of her forced servitude to him, she rejects the gifts for reasons neither of them understand.

So long as Seras continues to fight her nature uncompromisingly, there is no question that she will remain confused and unsettled, unable to find a place in her upside-down world. If she is able to discover a compromise between light and dark, things may finally settle into place for her. It remains to be seen, however, whether she can pull it off before her indecision destroys her existence.

Perhaps the most interesting event to happen to Seras within the boundaries of Hellsing is her meeting with the child-like vampire Helena. In *Order 08: Kill House*, this event explains more of her vampiric nature, and gives Seras a lot to think about. When Seras feels that she has nowhere else to turn later, she tries to meet with Helena again, only to find that Incognito had the same idea ... but with vastly different intent. Nevertheless, Helena manages to dispense some more vampiric wisdom to Seras before dying.

Following her second visit to Helena, Seras rushes to the Tower of London, trying to alert the Hellsing units of the trap into which they are walking. Her warning is not heard, and she arrives in time to see Peter Fargarson die at the hands of a sniper. Vowing revenge, she then goes back into combat against the SAS soldiers-turned-ghouls even though she was no longer a member of the Hellsing First Action Unit. Her zeal gets her into trouble as she tries to pass Arucard a clip of silver bullets during his battle with Incognito. Arucard warns her away, but she doesn't heed his commands and Incognito cuts her throat open.

After taking what would be a mortal wound for a human, Seras licks some blood from Arucard's mouth, but does not participate in the final battle. Seras is last shown cradling the wounded Integra.

WALTER DDOLLNEAZZ

Walter Ddollneazz is a former operative in the Hellsing Organisation. He has retired, and now is a retainer of the Hellsing Family. He performs the services of butler, major-domo, personal assistant, and bodyguard for Sir Integra as well as seeing to the day-to-day needs of the supernatural residents of Hellsing mansion. He is supposedly an older gentleman, but his long hair is still dark, drawn back into a low ponytail. His age could be anywhere between 60 and 90 years.

Walter is something of an enigma. He obviously has a long history with the Hellsing Organisation in general and the Hellsing family in specific, but what his specific job was or how long he did it is never discussed. The only clues exhibited take place in Episode 6, when he takes on Jan Valentine and an army of ghouls almost single-handedly, fighting with a pair of gloves that have lethal monowires strung between them. His movements are graceful, like a dancer or a martial artist, and he kills entire ranks of the ghouls in just moments.

During this battle, he states that he has "waged war against the true armies of the undead." Arucard also fondly calls him the "angel of death," much as one would use an old nickname. It seems clear that Walter was a specialist for the organisation at one time, probably nearly on par with Arucard. This would account for their unusually close behaviour, including sharing jokes (something Walter rarely does) and teasing Seras gently. It is clear, both in the scene described above in Episode 5 and in an exchange with Integra in Episode 2 that Walter does miss going into the field and fighting the undead face-to-face. He denies the allegation, but he was obviously very good at what he did. He seems at peace with the decision, but he is obviously pleased at the chance to go to battle again against the ghouls of the Valentine brothers. Later, he is tested by Boobanshee's invasion of the Hellsing Mansion, where he is placed under mind control and attacks Seras Victoria. Under the circumstances, Seras forgives him the next day. Mere days later, Walter is forced to pilot a helicopter — under fire from the British Military — to take Integra to the Tower of London. Integra falls from the helicopter and Walter carefully catches her with his monowire lines and is able to set her safely on the ground. Afterwards, he is unable to regain control of the helicopter, and it crashes to the ground. Walter is wounded, perhaps fatally.

Walter is good with computers and people, displaying a keen mind and an oddly compelling British upper-class sort of charisma. He serves as Integra's confidante and advisor on matters involving the Hellsing Organisation, even though he no longer holds any official rank. It is likely that he became the family's official retainer during Integra's father's time as the head of the Organisation. Integra likely grew up with Walter as an unofficial member of the household and has thus known him since she was a little girl. This would account for her singular trust in him.

Despite his violent past, Walter is really the humanising link for all the occupants of Hellsing mansion. He maintains a standard of civility and respect that is impossible not to honour, reminding the other inhabitants that humanity is as much a standard to maintain as a temporal condition.

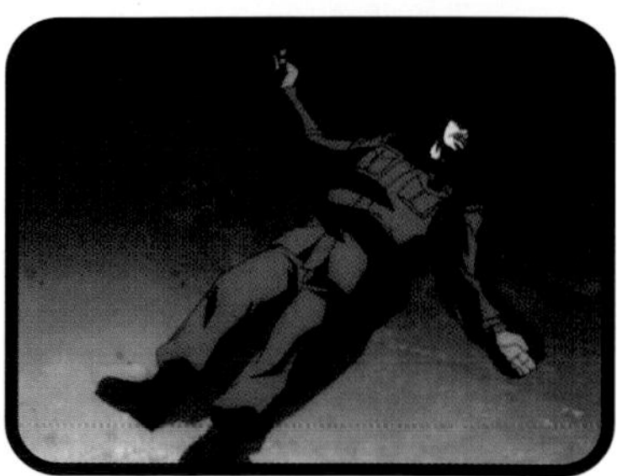

PETER FARGASON

Peter Fargason is the commander of the Hellsing Special Operations Unit. His rank is a mystery, as it is not specified in the any of the initial episodes. None of his subordinates address him as anything other than sir, and Sir Integra addresses him only as "Peter" or "Fargason," depending on the situation.

Peter is in charge of field operations for Hellsing and is always present on troop manoeuvres. He is also nominally in charge of Seras's training. Integra speaks with him regularly regarding the status of the men and women under his command, and he takes a personal interest in Seras's progress.

Fargason is under the direct command of Sir Integra Hellsing, and he treats her mostly as he would a military officer of superior rank, calling her "ma'am" or "sir" and obeying the directives she gives him. There is no evidence of any other dimension to their relationship, though it is obvious she relies on his experience and competence in commanding the Hellsing units. Other than Integra, Seras is the only one of the main characters with whom he has any specific interaction. Later, when he is forced to remove Seras Victoria from the Hellsing First Action Unit, he carries out this task with his usual military manner, not letting his slight friendship with Seras get in the way of business.

For all his talents and good qualities, Fargason also has very real flaws. His choice of Steadler as a replacement for Gareth is the result of one, namely a traditional soldier's willingness to see a sterling service record as a proof of character. With Fargason, if you have a good recommendation and have served in the right units, you can slip past his watchful eye under the haze of prior good acts. The same trick would never work with Integra, for example, but Fargason will let his guard down for someone who has ostensibly proven him or herself.

Overconfidence is Fargason's second flaw. In this case, however, the overconfidence is not in himself but in his troops. When dealing with Seras, he never lets her vampiric status become anything but a tactical asset. Privately, however, he admits to Seras in Episode 6 that he used to believe his men could handle almost any threat thrown at them just as well as the vampires could. While he saw the need for Arucard against powerful supernatural foes, he originally did not believe that the chipped vampires were a threat of the same magnitude.

Peter's television obituary reveals a few more details about his past. He was a former Army captain that served in the Gulf War, was decorated three times, and was honourably discharged following the Gulf War. Despite his achievements, his death is happy news to the British public, who are ignorant as to the actual nature of his work with The Hellsing Organisation.

Paladin Alexander Andersong

Alexander Andersong is a priest of Scottish descent, currently living in Rome. He is a member of the Vatican's secret bureau Section Thirteen, the Iscariot Organisation — a Catholic version of the Hellsing Organisation. He holds the title of paladin and possesses impressive regenerative powers thanks to unnamed technological processes. He is a very tall man who wears glasses, priestly robes and an ever-present trench coat.

Alexander appears in only three episodes of the series, namely *Sword Dancer*, *Duel*, and *Hellfire*. He appears to be Arucard's Vatican counterpart, and was sent into England specifically to retrieve the chipped vampire who died at a local college. He supersedes his authority and violates the Hellsing Organisation's jurisdiction to seek out Enrico Stivaletti, the chipped vampire.

He also engages Arucard and Seras in combat, anxious to carry out the mission statement of the Iscariot Organisation in as wide a mandate as possible. Only Integra's quick thinking, political pull, and her ability to make others bend to her will prevents Andersong from possibly destroying Arucard and Seras. The second time they meet, Alexander defeats Arucard temporarily, and only Arucard's quick resurrection saves Seras from certain doom. The final time the Paladin appears is during the last episode, as he observes the battle at the Tower of London.

The face-off between the Hellsing vampires and Andersong make it a certainty that any future meetings will result in a lethal contest. There is absolutely no love lost between them, and Integra has made it clear that she expects Arucard to hold his own against the priest, should it come to that. It is very obvious that Andersong considers his life's work to be a sacred calling. The very idea of vampires conducting the same type of activity is blasphemous to him, and something he actively works to prevent. Andersong even considers it just and righteous to murder humans working for the Hellsing Organisation, as demonstrated when he stabs Gareth Henderson in the back during the hospital mission.

Alexander possesses the ability to ward areas against supernatural vampiric powers. Although never stated, it is conceivable that the chipped nature of the instant vampires would circumvent this ward, possibly resulting in a nasty surprise for the priest. Andersong's predatory instincts would ensure, however, that his unfortunate error was never repeated. He holds an impressive knowledge of vampiric abilities and powers, including their weaknesses. He prefers melee combat to gun combat and uses blessed blades and prayer for his vampire-dispatching work.

It should be noted that Andersong was not designated specifically as Scottish in the original Japanese version of the anime. That was done for the dubbed English translation, an intriguing choice considering the centuries-old disagreement between Catholic Scots and Protestant English. Though that particular rift is less volatile now than it was in centuries past, it adds an additional depth to the enmity between Integra and Andersong.

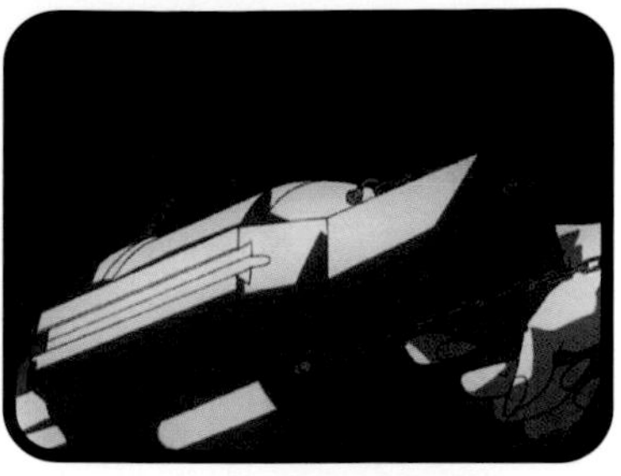

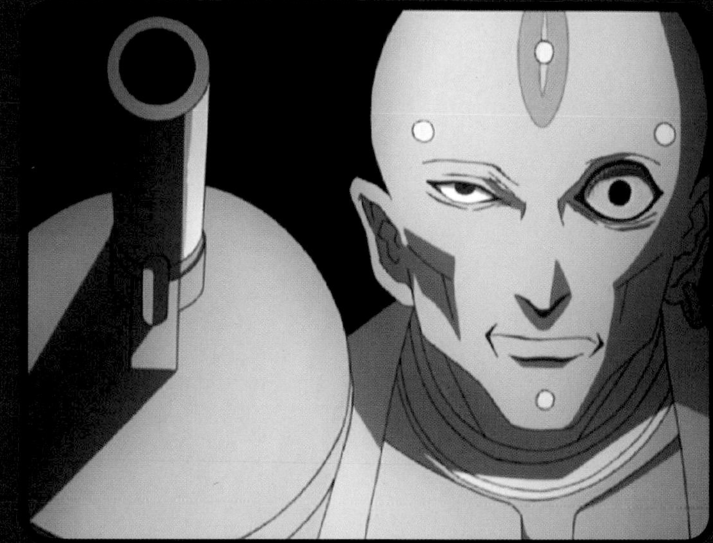

INCOGNITO

Incognito is the most powerful foe Arucard has ever encountered. His location of origin is unknown, although Arucard refers to his flechette rounds as "sorcery from the dark continent" at one point, perhaps indicating that Incognito is from Africa. It appears that until Incognito set foot on British soil, Arucard was not aware of his existence. However, Incognito certainly seemed to know all about the Hellsing Organisation and Arucard, executing a multi-pronged attack against both of them immediately after arriving in England.

Physically, Incognito is of above average height, and well muscled. He often wears a full-length tan-coloured jacket, although he is also seen naked, and genderless, on other occasions. His skin is a pale grey, and purple runes glow on his body when he uses his magical powers. He has multiple piercings; thick gold earrings, and studs in his chin, eyebrows, forehead, and chest. His left eye continually glows red. His body shape is unusual, most notably his head, which is extremely round on top but protrudes in a rather angular way at the back.

Incognito's supernatural powers appear to be on par with Arucard's, although he does not showcase much diversity in them. He obviously uses some sort of supernatural power to overcome, slay, and imprison the SAS forces at Bobhan Castle, but exactly how he does so is a mystery. His other powers are more direct. In the battle at London Tower, he uses laser-like attacks to cut Arcuard and Seras, and sends out a laser beam so powerful it slices right through the tower walls, sending them crashing to the ground.

Like Arucard, Incognito has a human master. This human master is never seen, but at one point Arucard refers to him as "Sett." In *Order 13: Hellfire*, Incognito claims that he is summoning the demon Sett, who manifests as a giant beam of blue light that rampages through London, leaving destruction in its wake.

Egyptian myth talks about Set — the god of strength, war, storms, foreign lands, and deserts. Some legends say Set sometimes appeared in the animal form of a greyhound, similar to the animal form that the chipped vampire Paul Wilson can assume. As time progressed, Set began to be associated more with evil, and a legend formed that involved him killing his brother Osisris — twice.

Arucard slays Incognito at the climax of *Hellsing*, impaling him on a spike of silver.

LUKE AND JAN VALENTINE

Luke and Jan Valentine are the owners and operators of an unnamed fetish club somewhere in London. They are also chipped vampires, the most powerful and connected ones shown in the city thus far. The brothers are obviously in contact with either the manufacturer or distributor of the chips or someone who is close to him or her.

Luke is well-dressed, with a thin build, long blond hair, and glasses. He looks almost as if he could be Integra's sibling and speaks with an educated tone. Jan is always casually dressed, with strange yellow eyes and multiple facial piercings. He tends to ramble and talks like a street thug. In their partnership, it is Luke who makes plans and runs the business end of things while Jan acts as the enforcer and works with their subordinates.

Luke and Jan's involvement with the Hellsing Organisation begins when one of their warning signs — a playing card with a symbol resembling the eye of Horus on it — finds its way back to them in the unwitting hands of an undercover government agent. Since the agent was carrying a cross, he was obviously a religious man — someone who would never wish to become a vampire.

By the time the brothers make their attack on Hellsing mansion, however, they possess all the pertinent information they need. They set up the events that lead to the calling of the Round Table meeting and are even certain where and when the meeting will be held. They know of Integra and the Hellsing Organisation, including the location of the headquarters. They possess knowledge of the ground and the house, the defenses that are to be expected, and the existence of Arucard. Luke specifically pursues the goal of fighting Arucard and destroying him, thus proving his superiority, while Jan is pleased simply to kill, turn people into ghouls, and eventually wipe out the entire Round Table. How the brothers received this information is not made clear initially, but their superior clearly has excellent intelligence-gathering capabilities.

The Valentine brothers are killed in the assault on Hellsing mansion. Luke meets his end at the hands of Arucard, ending up as little more than a bloodstain on some stairs. Jan dies by his own hand after being shot by Integra, setting himself on fire rather than reveal who sent the pair of them against Hellsing. It seems obvious, though, that despite the damage they did, the real danger to Hellsing and all its members is still out there.

Laura / Boobhanshee

Boobhanshee appears only in *Order 9: Red Rose Vertigo,* posing as Integra's sister Laura. Walter grants her access to the mansion while Integra is still at Bobhan Castle, and Integra meets with her in her office when she returns. Integra seems awkward throughout the meeting, as Laura talks about how the family from Avon is doing well.

Laura's presence in the mansion strikes Seras the wrong way; she has an odd feeling about things even before she sees Laura. After discovering that Laura and Integra do not look alike, she is even more suspicious. Seras tries to rush upstairs to see what's happening to Integra, but Walter — under the influence of some sort of mind control power — blocks her way.

Integra's questioning of Laura introduces some potential reasons behind her sudden invasion of the Hellsing mansion. She says that a girl named Laura was the victim of Karmilla Miraluca, and questions the vampire if that is her true name. Integra also calls her Boobhanshee, although it's not clear why she thinks that may be her name, nor is any history revealed.

As Laura talks, it is clear that she is working for someone else. She has instructions on how exactly to turn Integra into a ghoul. Although Laura does not reveal who she works for, Incognito reveals to Arucard — perhaps just a little too early, for Laura has not yet finished her work — that Arucard's master is dead. It seems clear that Boobhanshee is working for Incognito, although it is not known if she is working for him willingly. Additionly, she refers to the people giving her orders as "they," indicating that it may be Incognito and someone else — perhaps the traitor from the Knights of the Round Table, or (though quite unlikely) the Iscariot Organisation?

Boobhanshee's powers appear much more limited than either Arucard or Incognito. While she is able to deceive Walter and Integra, Seras senses that something strange is up almost as soon as she arrives back at the mansion, and Integra manages to partially break free of Boobhanshee's mental powers. When he arrives back at the mansion, Arucard easily disposes of Boobanshe with a single silver bullet. Boobhanshee may have managed to fool the occupants of the Hellsing mansion once, but she only had a single trick up her sleeve.

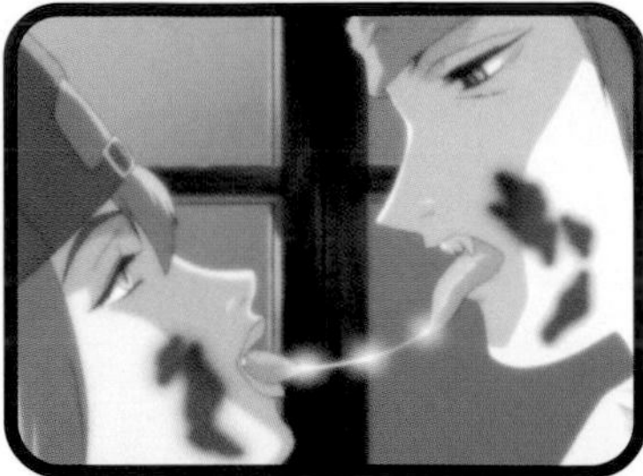

Lief and Jessica

Lief and Jessica are two thrill-killing, "Bonnie and Clyde" teenage vampires who go on a spree in the countryside near Birmingham. Under the belief that they must kill a set number of people in order to become more powerful, they set about murdering families, trashing houses and covering the walls in obscene and blasphemous graffiti before moving on to their next victims. The pair of killers believes themselves in love. They have no understanding of their own mortality, no concept of the cursed existence of the vampire. They only know or care that drinking blood gets them high and that they're willing to do whatever it takes for the next hit. It is possible that their belief in power from killing was given to them by the person who gave them the Freak chips, with the promise to upgrade them if they performed the assigned task. Arucard and Jessica kill the pair at the end of the second episode.

Enrico Stivaletti

Enrico Stivaletti is an attractive blond foreign student at an English college from Italy. Prior to Episode 3 where he appears, Enrico receives a Freak chip implant. He is young and impulsive and believes he can turn his gay lover, Mick, into an immortal vampire as well. Enrico accidentally drinks too much of Mick's blood, though, which kills his lover. Shortly after Mick's death, Enrico's actions are discovered. His body is brought to a hospital for examination. After Enrico escapes and kills a score of doctors and security officers, Hellsing responds and works to bring him down. Arucard eventually kills Enrico, using his gloved hand to impale the vampire through the heart from behind.

Priest

This individual from the first episode was assigned to the village of Cheddar, and was responsible for the deaths of countless victims during his reign of terror. His name was never mentioned, but in addition to the people who disappeared from the town, he killed a local police unit and over half of D-11, the London Police Authority's elite special ops unit. He was ready to embrace Seras as a vampire when Arucard stopped him, killing the priest and embracing Seras himself.

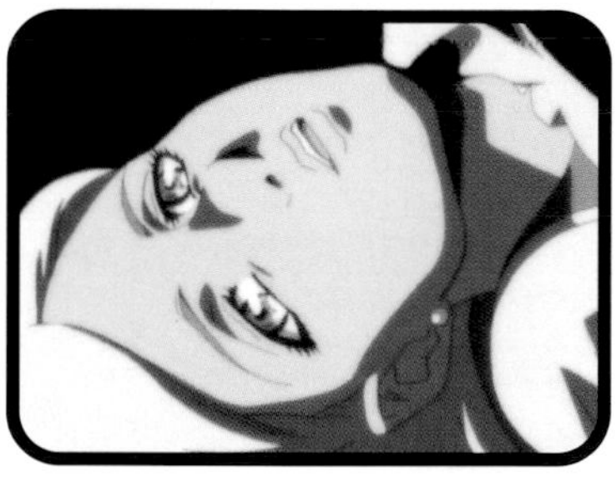

GARETH HENDERSON

Captain Gareth Henderson is the squad leader of Seras's unit during the point at which Seras is transferred to Hellsing. He is a crack shot and an effective leader, quickly integrating Seras into the unit as a whole. Paladin Andersong kills him at the hospital. He was shown in Episodes 2 and 3, and was replaced by Steadler in Episode 4.

KIM

Kim is an attractive blonde-haired woman who is featured in two Episodes, 2 and 4. Initially, she is the victim of an unsuccessful ghoul attack, resurfacing two episodes later as the television reporter who is chasing down the story of the Hellsing Organisation. The memory of her rescue at their hands does not engender gratitude in her, but instead awakens both greed and ambition. She possibly subverts Steadler into helping her. Kim's journalistic ambition blinds hèr to any sense of what might be inappropriate. Integra's realisation of this leads her to hand Kim over to Arucard for justice, who kills her by drinking her blood.

STEADLER

Steadler is introduced in Episode 4, *Innocent as a Human*. He is Captain Henderson's replacement, an ex-SAS operative with a spotless combat record. Steadler makes a poor captain, though, as is proven by his actions toward Seras during their first set of manoeuvres. Steadler insults Seras, picking on her relative inexperience, her gender, and her vampiric nature. He makes sexist comments that immediately alienate her and almost get him killed. Steadler sets out to undermine the Hellsing Organisation, feeding information to a reporter at a local TV station. He was involved in filming snuff films of vampires killing humans and trying to distribute the footage. He is arrested and sent off to await trial at the end of Episode 4.

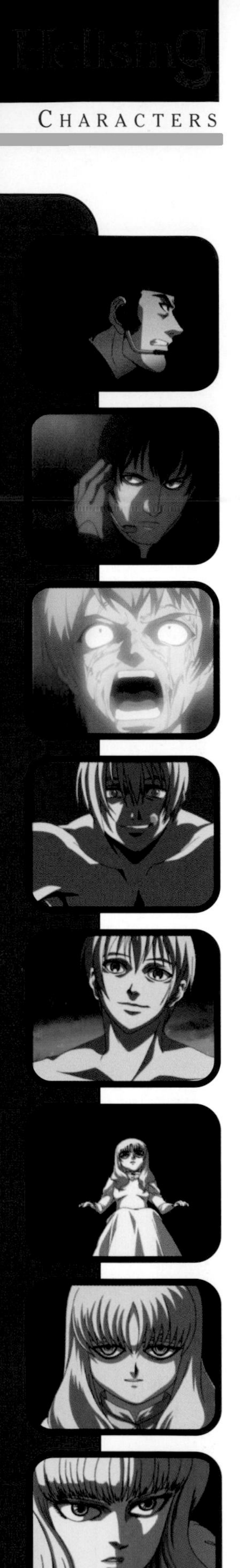

SERGEANT PICKMAN

Pickman is the lowest-ranking Hellsing soldier (aside from Seras) to whom Arucard is seen talking. The undead warrior seems to be rather respectful of Pickman, who joined the Hellsing First Action Unit as part of the widespread recruitment that took place after the Valentine brother's raid. His first major position is squad leader of the Bobhan Castle raid, although that mission is aborted early. He fights bravely through the London Tower assault, but he is eventually wounded by one of Incognito's ghouls. Unwilling to become a ghoul and wanting to die honourably for Hellsing, he asks Arucard to kill him. Arucard obliges.

PAUL WILSON

Paul is a young (23 years old) soldier assigned to the SAS unit that raids Bobhan Castle. Captured by Incognito, he is offered the choice of eternal life and is implanted with a Freak chip. Unlike the rest of the SAS soldifers, he does not join the unit that attacks the Hellsing Organisation at the Tower of London. Instead, he seems to stalk Seras — appearing first in her dreams, then by the side of the road at the Hellsing mansion, until finally he attacks her at the Tower of London. During the scuffle, he both turns into wolf-form and taunts her, telling her that she is no better than a ghoul, and tries to convince her to start a new life with him. Paul is finally killed when Seras detonates a Halcannon round between his teeth.

HELENA

Helena is a natural vampire in the body of a young child. Seras learns of her existence when Harry Anders from MI-5 asks Seras to accompany him to visit Helena. She lives alone in a rooftop apartment, although the only room shown is the library; perhaps it is the only room there, or perhaps she owns the whole building but keeps the entrance on the roof for privacy. Helena is not openly aggressive, but obviously does not approve of Seras's involvement with Hellsing. When she learns that Seras only deals with Freak chip vampires, and that her master is Arucard, she relents a little and gives Harry and Seras some information: she believes no British vampires were part of the Freak chip creation process.

Later in the series, Seras returns to Helena's apartment, only to find that Incognito has attacked her. Helena fights off Incognito long enough to tell Seras about a vampire's afterlife and how their essence travels through the heavens once their soul is separated from their body. After Helena dies, her apartment building burns to the ground.

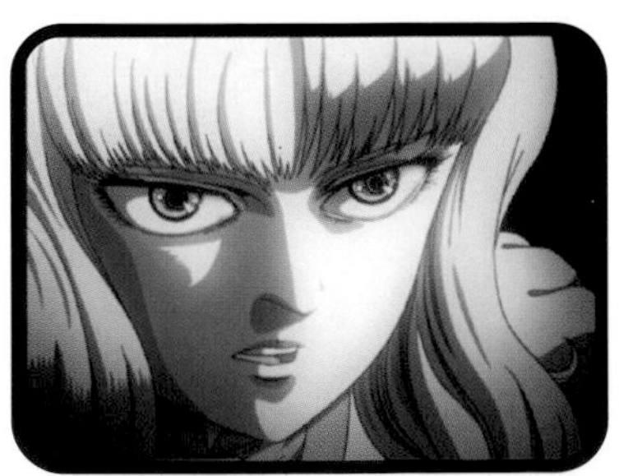

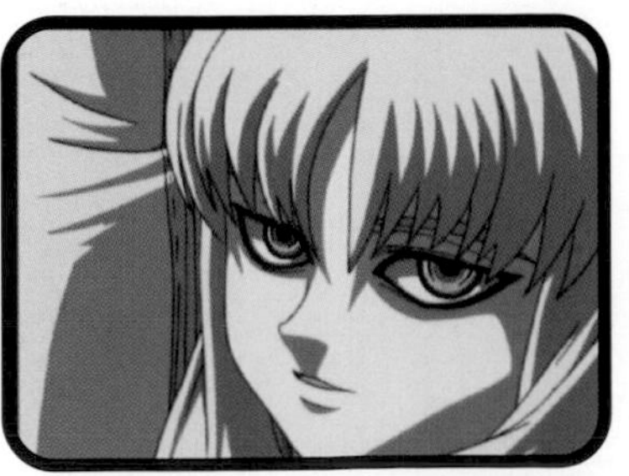

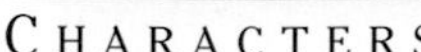

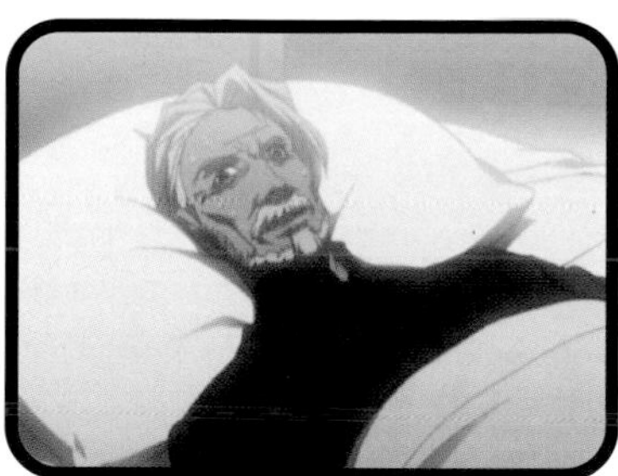

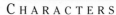

HARRY ANDERS

Harry Anders is one of two primary MI-5 agents in *Hellsing* (the other was last seen in *Order 4: Innocent as a Human*). In *Order 8: Kill House*, Harry visits Seras Victoria, off record, and takes her to meet the vampire Helena. He uses Seras as a shield to protect himself from Helena's power, while trying to find out more information about the Freak chip vampires and their origins. Helena mostly ignores Harry, expressing her anger and disgust that her and the other vampires are continually hunted, even though she claims they do no harm and just want to live peacefully.

Harry's car explodes as he drives away from Seras' apartment, after dropping her off. It is presumed that he is killed instantly in the explosion, but his death is not explored further in *Hellsing*.

SIR HELLSING (INTEGRA'S FATHER)

Integra's father is not given a first name in the short flashback of Integra's childhood. His physical appearance — a weathered face and grey hair — combined with his death of apparently natural causes indicate that he was likely in his 50s or even 60s when he died. He appears to be a well-educated man, proud of his family and his work, and he expects Integra to live up to that legacy. He chastises her when she shows up five minutes late for home schooling, but appears kind yet firm.

Sir Hellsing also had control of Arucard at one point and left him imprisoned in the mansion's dungeon for about twenty years. How he came to be Arucard's master is never mentioned.

Integra's mother — who we assume was her father's wife — is dead. Sir Hellsing was briefly survived by his brother, Richard.

RICHARD HELLSING

Perhaps the rightful heir to the Hellsing Organisation, Sir Hellsing's younger brother Richard is passed over, and the Hellsing Organisation was given to Integra. Anticipating this, Richard had been planning for years to kill the young woman and assume control of Hellsing. Not much else is known about Richard. After Sir Hellsing's death, he assembles a group of four men as his bodyguards, and they attempt to hunt Integra down. Integra overhears their plotting and frees Arucard from his prison below the Hellsing mansion. In the struggle that ensues, Arucard kills the four bodyguards. It is unclear if Richard was killed in that struggle, and if so, by whom. It seems most likely, though, that Integra killed her own uncle, as opposed to having him imprisoned.

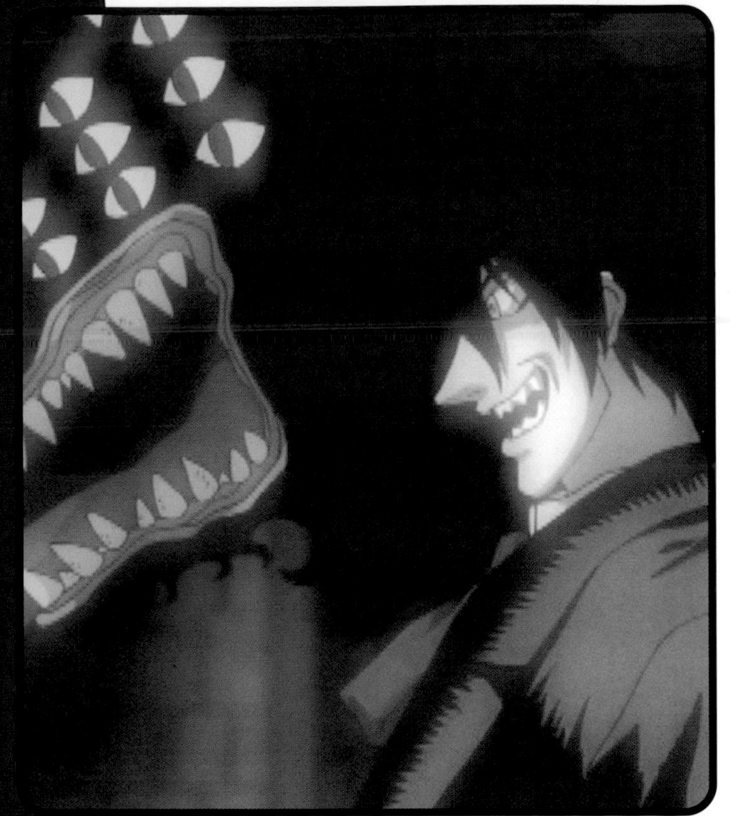

SETTING AND WORLD OF HELLSING

The *Hellsing* series is set in England, a fitting and traditional backdrop for a vampire story. Used by such varied authors as Le Fanu, Yarbro and, of course, Stoker, London's fog-banked streets and narrow alleys lend themselves to the contemplation of creatures that walk the night, both human and inhuman. Even in our days of modern conveniences and commonplace electric lighting, sometimes the contrast only serves to make the shadows deeper and more frightening. And with the backdrop of London's stolid, unchanging face before us, we are allowed to sink into the setting easily, like greeting an old friend, and get right on to the business at hand.

London's streets, alleyways and manor houses allow for a dizzying array of settings to be used, all in the same locale. Rich to poor, seedy to extravagant are all equally available and realistic. Only a few miles separate extremes of wealth, class and privilege, making for a smorgasbord of gothic thrills that can please almost any fancy.

The series does not limit itself, however, to the urban streets of London. The episodes in the *Hellsing* series take place all around England, from Coventry to Cheddar, Birmingham to Camden Town. The bucolic countryside of Cheddar sees undead wandering its woods and vampiric priests in its gothic cathedrals. The highways and single-family dwellings around Birmingham see bloody rampages and murdered children. The small-town idyll of Coventry sees death. As the story deals heavily with the failings of human nature and the destruction those failings can cause, so it is that nowhere touched by man, even in the slightest, is safe from being touched by man's darker side.

Still, London possesses something that none of the other areas mentioned can match; untold masses of humanity. Only in London is it feasible to create armies of ghouls and have no one the wiser for a time. Only in London can vampires dressed in anachronistic fashions walk the nighttime streets without causing comment. Crime and virtue can live cheek by jowl in such a place, with neither being given undue attention. Combine that fact with easy access to the unquestioned seat of power for the whole nation, and that is why London serves as the setting for the majority of the first half of the series.

Hellsing is a very modern series, and it chooses a modern-day time frame. There are no indications to say exactly what decade the show was set, an omission that was certainly intentional. The timeframe is certainly no earlier than 1990, and not very far in the future, if at all. The only futuristic piece of technology is the Freak chip — an aberration which can easily be explained away in an alternate timeline.

HELLSING HISTORY: ONE POSSIBLE INTERPRETATION

Speculation: *Hellsing*'s history mirrors much of our own from all indications. The primary difference from the point of view of the story is in changes from the Bram Stoker novel *Dracula*, which seems to be included in the Hellsing timeline as actual events that took place.

In *Dracula*, the characters of Jonathan Harker, Mina Harker, Lord Godalming (Arthur Holmwood), Dr. Jack Seward, Quincy Morris and Dr. Abraham Van Helsing combine forces to defeat the plans of the vampire Count Dracula and destroy him, thus saving Mina's life.

Van Helsing is a Catholic of Dutch or German descent who comes to England through the request of his former student, Jack Seward. He is an older man whose only son has died. His wife is mad and locked in an asylum. By the laws of the time, he cannot divorce her or marry another, leaving him alone and childless. Though they must fight through harrowing adventures, at the end of the book, Count Dracula is destroyed and turned to dust. In the prologue, it is stated that they have no original documents left to them, thus their story can never be made public with any hope of belief — an ending they can be content with now that the danger has passed away. Obviously, these points have no bearing in the *Hellsing* series.

Instead, what if Helsing was able to remarry an English woman and start the Hellsing line? His son from his first marriage either survived or he was able to have more children. He and his companions were obviously not only believed, but also heralded as heroes. He or one of his descendants was granted a knighthood. The family line also acquired wealth and an estate, though whether this was granted with the title or gained through another means are unknown.

Plot points were also changed regarding the Count, first and foremost being that he was not destroyed. Somehow he overcame his purely predatory nature, as shown in the novel, or else he was bound to serve a greater good by other outside forces. Instead of having his plans to move to London thwarted, he relocates here under the auspices of the Hellsing family. The creation of ghouls is also something created for the series that did not exist in Stoker's imagination, though other modern-day vampire literature may have provided that inspiration.

It is also clear that vampirism is much wider spread in *Hellsing* than it is in the 1897 novel. In England alone, there were enough occurrences that the Hellsing Organisation came into being. It is possible that the Organisation also consulted for nations outside the British Empire, but there is no evidence for either conclusion. In either case, Hellsing and his family did not cease their investigations into the undead with the capture or destruction of Dracula. Instead, they founded an institution on the very practice, turning it into a science instead of a guessing game. At some point, the "family business" became a full-fledged special ops group and was co-opted by Her (or His) Majesty's government under the auspices of national security.

Of course, the series never reveals the true origins of the Hellsing Organisation — this is simply speculation.

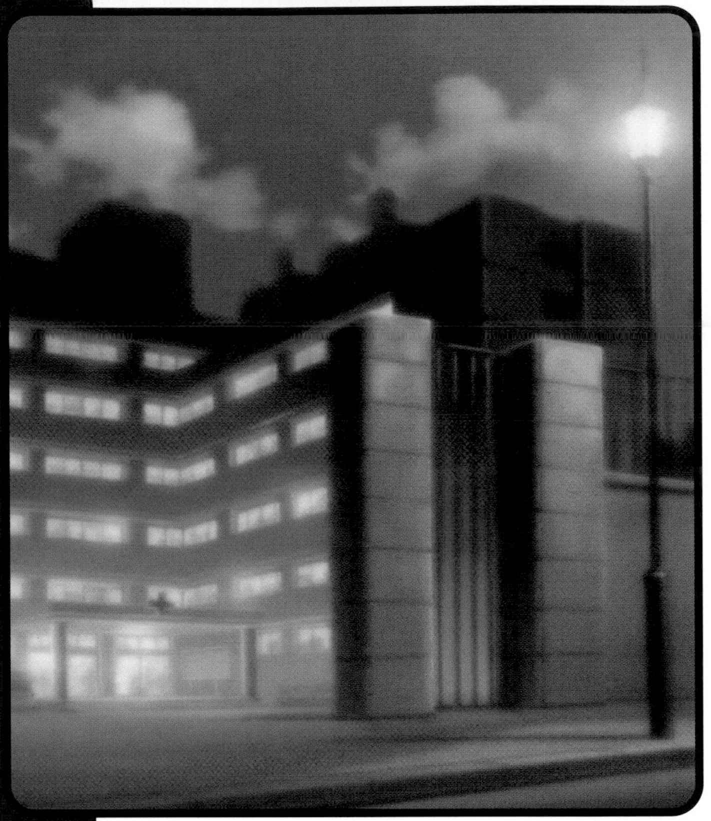

LOCATIONS

COVENTRY

Coventry is a city in the West Midlands of central England, not far from Birmingham. It is an industrial centre as well, known for producing motor vehicles, aircraft engines, textiles and bricks. It has a population of around 300,000 individuals. In addition to its industrial side, Coventry is home to a number of institutions of higher learning. Some of the more prestigious of these are the University of Warwick and Coventry University.

Coventry itself has a notable history, including being the home of the legendary (but still very real) Lady Godiva. In the Middle Ages, Coventry was considered Britain's "Third City." It was bombed heavily by the Germans in World War II but has largely been rebuilt.

Coventry is mentioned in Episode 4: *Innocent as a Human*. It is the location of a mission in which the shooting of a Hellsing operative was filmed. Steadler later assists in the distribution of this footage on the internet.

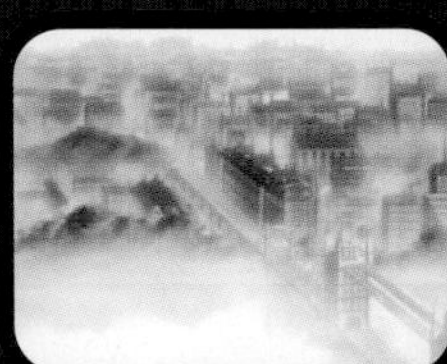

LONDON

London is the seat of British government and the capital of the United Kingdom. It has a population of roughly 7 million inhabitants, making it by far the largest city in Europe — a distinction it has maintained since the 17th century. It is one of the world's major financial and cultural capitals, making it recognisable nearly the world over.

London is very spread out for a European city, roughly 30 miles in diameter at its widest point. The character and culture tends to divide into distinct sections, most of which were once separate villages that were swallowed up by London's ever-increasing sprawl. They still maintain their individual identities, however, and it is this that gives London so much of its character and charm.

London is the home of the Hellsing Organisation, which is headquartered in Hellsing mansion and the family's surrounding gated estate. The estate's location in the city is not known, but it is certain that it is located within the confines of that city — close enough that Luke Valentine's claim of it being included on a "walking tour" of the city was not immediately laughed away.

Much of the action of the series also takes place in London, with at least part of each episode being set there and all of episodes four, five and six. It is in Camden Town in North London that Kim and Steadler set up the rigged broadcast of the Hellsing Organisation's activities. The booby-trapped warehouse is also in London, and the Valentine brothers' club is in a well-travelled entertainment district. The London Police Authority is the arm of law enforcement within the city, and they work closely with the Hellsing Organisation on cases that indicate the activities of the undead.

BIRMINGHAM

Birmingham is the second largest city in England and a major industrial centre. It is located in the West Midlands, central England. It is a hub of many different types of heavy industry, including metal goods, rubber products, electrical equipment, glass, chemicals and coal mining. A network of highways and railroads serve the city, meaning that it acts as a crossroads of sorts for travellers from across Britain.

Given its focus on industry, Birmingham has a heavy percentage of blue-collar workers. The majority of its inhabitants are middle-class, working-class families and young single adults. It is a growing city with a population of over one million inhabitants. It was heavily bombed in World War II, but has been mostly rebuilt at this point.

Birmingham appears briefly as the setting for much of the atrocities seen in episode two, Club M. The two teenagers, Lief and Jessica, are working-class kids who are probably from the area. They use the highways running around and through Birmingham as their own private thrill part, playing chicken with semi-trucks and weaving in and out of traffic. They also go on a rampage, slaughtering whole families in the area, drinking the blood then using the remainder to write blasphemous and obscene graffiti on the walls of the houses. Arucard and Seras travel there along with the Hellsing troops to deal with the young vampires, setting up a roadblock on a major highway in order to trap them.

CHEDDAR VILLAGE

Cheddar Village is a small town in Somerset county in southwestern England. It is known primarily for being the original home of cheddar cheese, which is named after the settlement. The town itself takes its name from Cheddar Gorge, a spectacular nearby canyon.

Cheddar is primarily a rural community with the entire county known mainly for its dairying and cider making. The countryside is pleasant, with wooded areas and a central lowland surrounded by ranges of hills.

The *Hellsing* series begins in Cheddar Village, with the arrival of a mysterious and disturbing priest. The first episode is set almost entirely in the wilderness surrounding the village and in the village church. It is there that Seras manages to survive her first encounter with the undead, and there as well that Arucard embraces her after the vampiric priest is killed.

LONDON LOCALES

Locations around London and the rest of the British Isles are used as dramatic venues in *Hellsing*. Some of the more interesting ones are listed below, along with details about their appearances in the series and some real life facts. World Wide Web addresses for many of the locations are listed on page 112.

THE NATIONAL GALLERY

The National Gallery was built in the 19th century, and remains open to this day. There are presently 3,200 paintings in the gallery and each year between four and five million people visit. This makes it an unlikely place for the leaders of powerful rival organisations to be holding a heated meeting, but nonetheless Sir Integra Wingates Hellsing and Enrico Maxwell meet there in *Order 7: Duel.*

While it may be expected that the painting Integra is viewing before the confrontation with Enrico Maxell and Father Renaldo has some significance, research indicates that it is actually a fictitious piece of art ... or perhaps just an incredibly obscure one.

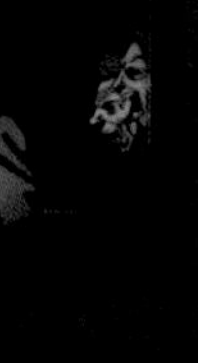

LONDON UNDERGROUND

The London Underground, also known as "The Tube," was first built in 1863. Over three million individual trips are taken on it each day. There are over 200 active train stations in the network as of 2003, and over 40 abandoned "ghost" stations that can still be seen and possibly accessed from some locations. The specific train stations mentioned in the series do exist, though it seems that the real life station "Queensway" is renamed "Queens Gate" in *Hellsing*.

In *Order 7: Duel*, Arucard and Andersong battle in the London Underground, first inside the train cars, then on the tracks. A fight of epic proportions between such powerful rivals could have had major consequences in such an enclosed area — injuring or killing civilians, damaging property, or even bringing the underground down on top of them!

KENSINGTON GARDENS

One of the Royal Parks, the Kensington Gardens are located close to the Queensway tube station and therefore, near the "Queens Gate" station in *Hellsing*. These gardens, first formed in 1689, are not seen during the series, but they could provide an attractive backdrop for both clandestine meetings and dramatic combat.

The Diana, Princess of Wales Memorial Playground was added to Kensington Gardens in June 2000 and a seven-mile Memorial Walk connects Kensington Gardens to Hyde Park, Green Park, and St Jame's Park.

THE TOWER OF LONDON

Located on the Thames River, The Tower of London has been a part of London's history for over 900 years. Despite the name, The Tower of London is actually a group of buildings and towers about 13 acres large. Previously a prison and a royal residence, in modern times the Tower is primarily a tourist attraction, but Yeoman Warders (more colloquially known as "Beefeaters") and their families still live within its walls. Yeoman Warders are all Extraordinary Members of the Queen's Bodyguard and are former members of Her Majesty's Forces; they must have served at least 22 years and have an honourable service record. The tower is also under military guard with units from the regiments that also guard Buckingham Palace and St James's Palace.

The Crown Jewels are stored and displayed in the Tower, though many other British institutions — The Mint and The Record House, to name two — have been moved out of the tower (primarily due to lack of space) in recent centuries. Weekly services in the Chapel Royal of St Peter ad Vincula, located inside the tower are open to the public every Sunday (excluding August and during the annual London Marathon). If visitors apply for tickets in advance, they may also watch the daily Ceremony of the Keys, which has been performed nightly for over 700 years.

Beauchamp Tower, featured prominently in *Hellsing* was built in the late 13th Century, and became a home to high-ranking prisoners. It stands three stories tall and was one of the first towers where bricks were used extensively, instead of stone. The tower draws its name from Thomas Beauchamp, Earl of Warwick, a prisoner in the late 14th century. Today, the upper chambers of Beauchamp Tower are filled with the inscriptions that generations of prisoners left behind.

The epic battle between Arucard and Incognito leaves London Tower in a state of disarray. Many of the individual towers are destroyed, and falling rubble lays waste to the smaller buildings below. It can only be assumed that the Queen would move quickly to repair the tower and bring the people responsible to justice — something that comes true when the Knights of the Round Table traitor is found and punished.

MAJOR ORGANISATIONS

The Hellsing Organisation is really a para-military operation, complete with all the paraphernalia that goes along with that. Its existence, while not common knowledge among the citizenry at large, is not surprising to those in the know. It begs the question of how widespread this sort of organisation is among governments in the *Hellsing* universe. Is it bordering on a conspiracy-theory setting where every powerful group holds its own personal strike force, or does it seem unremarkable because the Hellsing Organisation is an established entity that has been around for roughly a century (though in English history, that is still little more than a footnote)?

The only other similar group mentioned in the Hellsing series is the Iscariot Organisation, which is linked to the Vatican and thus a special ops group run by the Catholic Church. They seem to be given free reign outside of England on the European continent, or perhaps only in primarily Catholic nations. It seems a likely inference, then, that not every nation has its own undead-fighting group on hand. There is no mention of what occurs in the nations of North America, South and Central America, Africa, Asia or Australia. According to vampire lore, areas where the traditional cultures did not bury their dead would be less troubled by supernatural vampiric powers, so it may be that some places have no need for this type of policing organisation whatsoever.

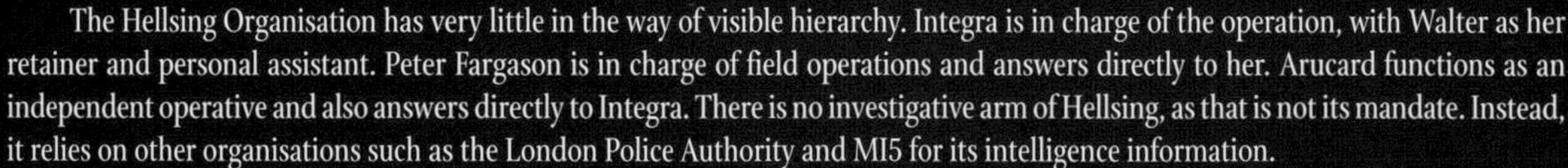

THE HELLSING ORGANISATION

When describing the Hellsing Organisation to the Round Table conference, Integra states that "the mission of the Hellsing Organisation is to end all Earthly activity of non-human creatures." That succinct phrase sums up the Hellsing Organisation well, because everything about the group is directly geared toward terminating those unlucky enough to fall within its sights.

The Hellsing Organisation has very little in the way of visible hierarchy. Integra is in charge of the operation, with Walter as her retainer and personal assistant. Peter Fargason is in charge of field operations and answers directly to her. Arucard functions as an independent operative and also answers directly to Integra. There is no investigative arm of Hellsing, as that is not its mandate. Instead, it relies on other organisations such as the London Police Authority and MI5 for its intelligence information.

Outside of the upper administrative levels, there are at least two companies of special forces troops to carry out assignments. It is unlikely there are more than three companies, but it is impossible to determine the exact number with any accuracy from the information in the series, due to high personnel turnover and the fact that the only troops seen with any regularity are with Seras's unit. The other squads and units are never differentiated.

Hellsing is actually a small agency, likely employing no more than 300 individuals at any given time. The Hellsing estate is sufficient to serve as both operational and living quarters for the entire Organisation at any given time, including the servants in the house. This is possible due to the narrow scope of their mission — which explains Integra's refusal to take on any further investigative responsibilities in pursuing the artificial vampires. The Hellsing Organisation simply lacks the manpower to take on such a task.

The supposedly secret Hellsing Organisation comes under fire from multiple sources throughout the series. Early on, a double-crossing soldier — Captain Steadler — attempts to expose them to the world, but he is caught before too much damage is done. Almost immediately after, chipped-vampire freaks Jan and Luke Valentine — along with an army of ghouls — raid the Hellsing Mansion, killing a majority of their troops. As the paramilitary organisation rushes to rebuild their ranks, the Iscariot Organisation threatens them, but a new and more deadly threat arrives from parts unknown: Incognito. The vampire Incognito puts the master plan to destroy Hellsing into motion, starting by capturing over sixty SAS soldiers and turning them into ghouls. Shortly thereafter, the vampire Boobanshee infiltrates the Hellsing Mansion, posing as Integra's sister, and attempts to kill Integra and turn her into a ghoul. Arucard's timely intervention saves Integra's life, but she is left weakened from the attack and does not regain full strength for the duration of the series.

With Integra recovering, the Knights of the Round Table hold a meeting without her. One of the members betrays Integra and the Round Table, leading her to believe that the Queen will be visiting the Hellsing Mansion to perform an unnamed ceremony. Hellsing operatives are sent to defend the London Tower from the SAS agents-turned-ghouls, but the British public is told that the Queen is at the Tower — and that Hellsing is attacking her! This brings the British Military down on Hellsing, placing them between a rock and a hard place! At the Tower of London, many Hellsing soldiers are killed, including Peter Fargason and Seargent Pickman. Despite the odds, Arucard manages to defeat Incognito at the Tower, and though the Hellsing Organisation is partially revealed to the world, they still emerge victorious.

Despite the victory, the Hellsing Organisation suffered great losses throughout the series. In addition to personnel losses, the Hellsing Mansion was badly damaged by the Valentine Brother's attack, and they appeared to lose some armoured transport vehicles at the Tower of London. More importantly, though, they have been nationally — probably internationally — exposed, and the veil of secrecy under which they used to operate lost, perhaps forever.

Although Hellsing was a secret organisation known only to the Knights of the Round Table and associated people, it is obvious that vampires such as Helena and Boobanshee were aware of the organisation and what it stood for. It is, after all, hard to remain a secret organisation when you are dealing death to supposed immortal creatures, and when you have two of them under your employ. It can be assumed that all true vampires are aware of the Hellsing Organisation, and likewise Hellsing is aware of them. Why Hellsing does not appear to be pursuing the more powerful vampires is a mystery, although it is likely that they do not see the older solitary vampires as a threat. The younger Freak chip vampires do not obey any vampiric codes or morals and thus present a more direct and overt threat towards national security.

KNIGHTS OF THE ROUND TABLE

The Round Table is a secret order of Knighthood, ostensibly appointed by the Queen of the United Kingdom and named for the legendary order created by King Arthur. The purpose of the Round Table is to protect the Empire against those who would harm her, whether the threat is internal or external. It is unclear whether the round table conference is a private group or one officially sanctioned by the government.

The conference consists of the chief officers of agencies involved in national security and has a total of ten members. King Arthur's round table was designed to be round so that all places at it would be equal, but there are no indications that modern round table conference has the same lofty goal.

The round table conference only meet rarely, since the members are all very important in their own fields; placing them all together at any one time is a large security risk. Only desperate measures can induce them to call an impromptu meeting, but once the meeting is called they all must answer. The only identified individuals on the board are Sir Islands, Sir Penwood, Chief or MI5, and Integra.

Sir Islands seems to be the mediating force among the conference members. His manner of speaking would seem to indicate that he is in charge of running the meetings or perhaps simply has a great deal of seniority. His organisation or affiliation is unknown.

Sir Penwood is antagonistic toward Integra, though Islands possesses enough power to rein him in as necessary. Penwood is in charge of information control, suggesting that he is affiliated with the Ministry of Media Management to which Walter refers to in Episode Four.

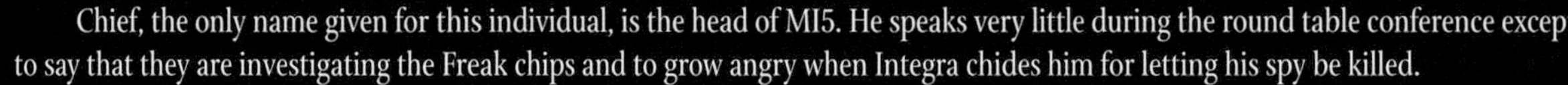

Chief, the only name given for this individual, is the head of MI5. He speaks very little during the round table conference except to say that they are investigating the Freak chips and to grow angry when Integra chides him for letting his spy be killed.

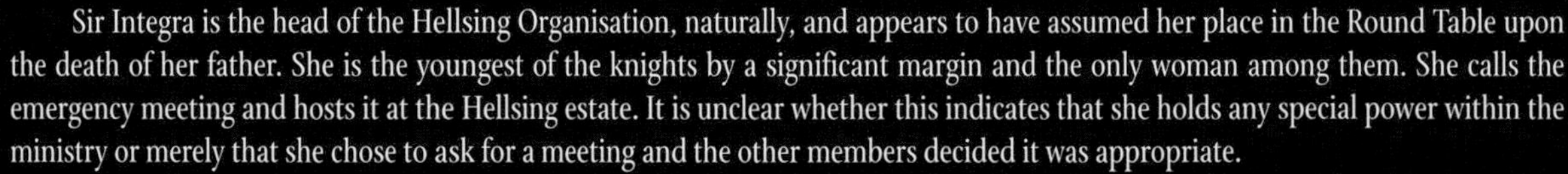

Sir Integra is the head of the Hellsing Organisation, naturally, and appears to have assumed her place in the Round Table upon the death of her father. She is the youngest of the knights by a significant margin and the only woman among them. She calls the emergency meeting and hosts it at the Hellsing estate. It is unclear whether this indicates that she holds any special power within the ministry or merely that she chose to ask for a meeting and the other members decided it was appropriate.

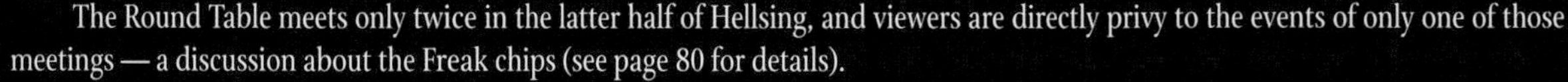

The Round Table meets only twice in the latter half of Hellsing, and viewers are directly privy to the events of only one of those meetings — a discussion about the Freak chips (see page 80 for details).

One of the members of the Round Table betrays all the other members — and Queen and Country — late in the series, trying to lure Hellsing into certain defeat at the Tower of London and reveal Hellsing to the public at large. While they do succeed in revealing Hellsing to the public, they are later caught and found guilty of treason. Despite this, the identity of the traitor is not revealed; for an exploration into the known members of the Knights of the Round Table and their potential to be the traitor, see page 78.

OTHER ORGANISATIONS

MI-5, The Iscariot Organisation, the SAS, the British Military, and the Royal Family all play important roles throughout *Hellsing*. Because the Knights of the Round Table traitor is never revealed (see page 78), it is possible that some of the organisations may have had a much greater role behind the scenes.

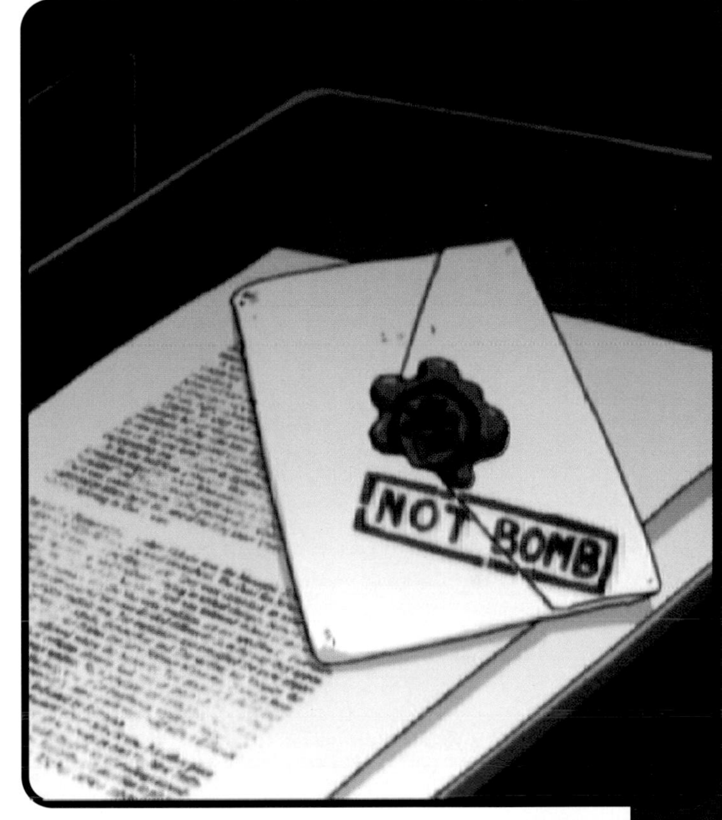

THE ISCARIOT ORGANISATION AND THE VATICAN

Hellsing's primary competitor is the Iscariot Organisation, a secret group that is headquartered in Rome and has a similar mission. The Vatican backs the secret bureau Section 13, the Iscariot Organisation. It appears to be composed of priests and other officials in the Catholic hierarchy, including at least one archbishop.

Paladin Alexander Andersong gives us the mission statement of Iscariot in Episode 3. "Our mission," he said, "is to punish any heretic who would deny the word of God. We will crush your unholy body, and salt the earth with your dust. Amen." While this is undoubtedly paraphrased in the heat of the moment, it highlights the differences between Iscariot and Hellsing.

Hellsing is pledged to support a Protestant government, and thus largely leaves interpretations of God and his Word aside. Its primary goal is simply to eradicate non-human or inhuman monsters that prey on humanity. God's influence in Hellsing is largely left unspoken, limited to the silver cross that is the symbol of the organisation, the blessed bullets used by Arucard, and the short formulaic prayers muttered at debriefings and on missions.

Iscariot operatives, on the other hand, carry God as both a weapon and a shield, solid in their belief that their opponent is not just a monster, but a sacrilegious, heretical monster. They are priests, sanctified in the Catholic Church, and it is unlikely that lay people or parishioners are allowed to even know of the group, much less participate. Far from being unspoken, God and their beliefs in the sacred righteousness of their actions are in their every speech.

Aside from the public face of the Vatican, which is well documented elsewhere, little is known about its interaction with Iscariot. The Pope's level of involvement is a complete mystery as is the level of knowledge regarding Iscariot within the Vatican itself.

Hellsing and Iscariot are fiercely competitive, especially if their paths cross on English soil. Ostensibly they are working toward the same goals, but given Hellsing's long-time affiliation with Arucard, it is unlikely the operatives view it that way.

Only three members of the Vatican's special operations division are revealed in *Hellsing*: Enrico Maxwell, his assistant Father Renaldo, and the technologically-infused combat machine Paladin Alexander Andersong. It is unknown whether the Iscariot Organisation has anything to do with bringing Incognito to England. Paladin Alexander Andersong observes the final fight between Arucard and Incognito at the Tower of London, but he does not intervene. The Paladin duels with Arucard in (appropriately enough) *Order 7: Duel* — the same episode in which Enrico Maxwell tells Integra that Hellsing must clean up the Freak chips or the Iscariot Organisation will destroy Hellsing.

The SAS

The British Special Air Service plays a small role in *Order 9: Red Rose Vertigo.* They order Hellsing to withdraw from Bobhan Castle, but the entirety of the SAS unit is then captured and turned into ghouls by Incognito. It is unknown whether Incognito somehow manipulated the SAS into showing up so he could capture them all. Strangely, the SAS makes no attempt to exact revenge upon Incognito, indicating that perhaps someone higher up at the SAS sacrificed the unit at Bobhan Castle to aid Incognito.

The British Military and Secret Service

The exact units and divisions of the British Military and Secret Service involved in Hellsing are not explained, but both organisations get involved defending Queen and Country when it is believed that Hellsing is attacking the Tower of London. Secret Service forces attempt to apprehend Integra at the Hellsing Mansion, and British Military pursue Integra and Walter in helicopters. At the Tower, a sniper shoots Peter Fargason dead, after he demands that British Military soldiers at the scene stand down. They appear to do so, but whether they are standing down to lower his guard or because they believe Hellsing is in the right is unknown.

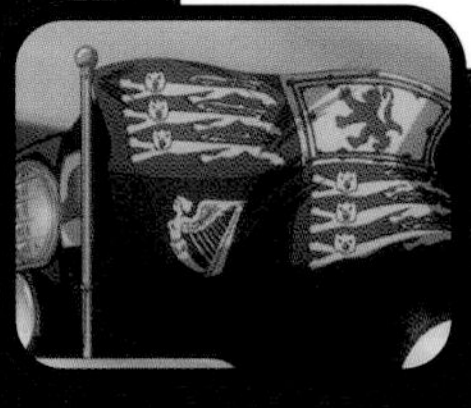

The Royal Family

The Royal Family and the Queen are never directly seen in *Hellsing*. While The Queen is rumoured to be visiting both The Tower of London and the Hellsing Mansion, she shows up at neither. Both rumours are carefully constructed lies — the first, towards the British population (to make them believe that the Hellsing Organisation is attacking the Queen) and the second towards the Hellsing Organisation (to make them believe it is safe to defend the Tower of London, and to occupy Integra at the Hellsing Mansion).

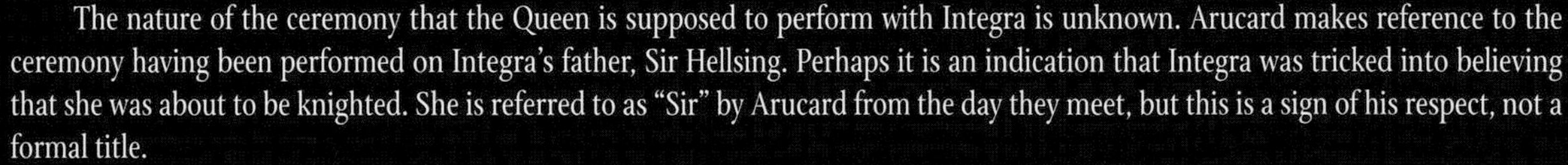

The nature of the ceremony that the Queen is supposed to perform with Integra is unknown. Arucard makes reference to the ceremony having been performed on Integra's father, Sir Hellsing. Perhaps it is an indication that Integra was tricked into believing that she was about to be knighted. She is referred to as "Sir" by Arucard from the day they meet, but this is a sign of his respect, not a formal title.

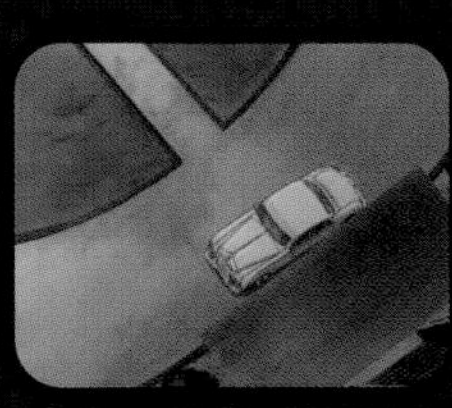

LAW ENFORCEMENT

Three areas of British law enforcement are focused on in the series. First is the London Police Authority (LPA), who deals with mundane crime within the limits of the city of London. They will also occasionally assist other bureaus in operations outside the city where the local law enforcement is not capable of providing adequate help.

The second group is the Hellsing Organisation, which exists outside the auspices of the LPA. They are a special operations group whose sole purpose to seek out and destroy the undead — infiltration, as the MI5 agents in episode four tell Seras. They are typically called in by the LPA when a case seems to warrant the Hellsing Organisation's special touch.

The third group is MI5, the Security Service of the United Kingdom. MI5s purpose is "to protect national security from threats such as terrorism, espionage and the proliferation of weapons of mass destruction, to safeguard the economic well-being of the UK against foreign threats, and to support law enforcement agencies in preventing and detecting serious crime," as per the MI5 web site (http://www.mi5.gov.uk/index.htm).

For the purposes of the *Hellsing* series, MI5 agents handle investigation and evaluation of evidence in cases of organised crime and other high-level threats. It's an MI5 agent that is killed by the Valentine brothers and dumped in the Thames. The head of MI5 is also a Knight of the Round Table, though his name is never specified.

Together, the three agencies are responsible for handling all mundane, foreign and supernatural crime that occurs both in the city of London and Britain as a whole. Unfortunately, professional pride and political ambition frequently keep the relationships between the agencies from being as harmonious as they might otherwise be. The working relationship between MI5 and the Hellsing Organisation is particularly fractious, due in no small part to competitive instincts between operatives. Each seems to feel that their areas and jurisdictions are sacrosanct. While that may have been true in the past, the technological nature of the Freak chip as well as the organised force behind it are causing the activities of the two groups to butt heads. Given the possible infiltration of at least one of the two agencies by the Freak suppliers, it is unlikely that this conflict will end peacefully any time soon.

While MI-5 has a seat on the Round Table, they as an organisation do not directly come into contact with the Hellsing Organisation. MI-5 investigator Harry Anders meets with Seras Victoria and the vampire Helena in *Order 8: Kill House,*, but he claims the meeting is not MI-5 sanctioned. Shortly after the meeting, Harry's car explodes, ending the direct involvement of any MI-5-related characters with Hellsing.

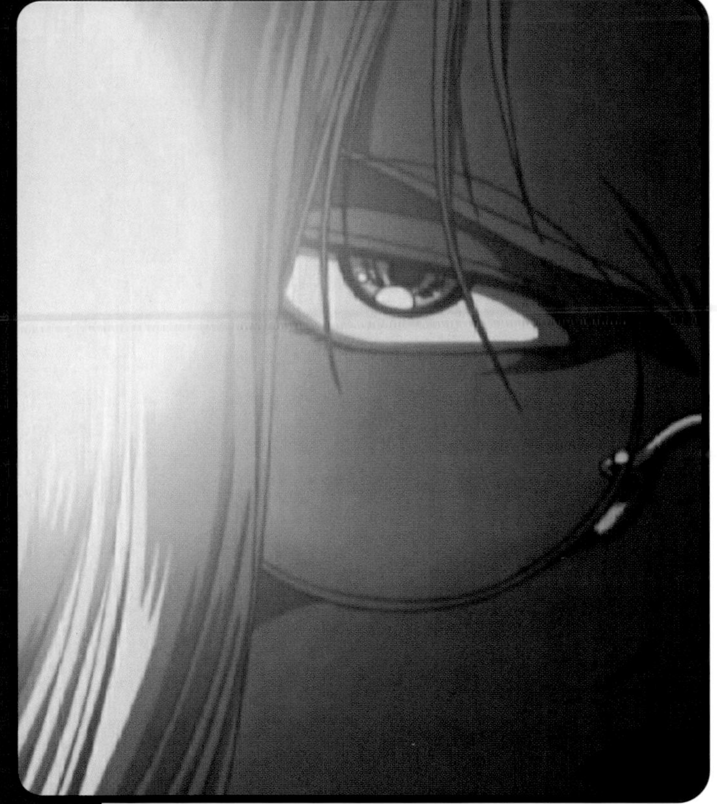

HELLSING MYSTERIES

WHO WAS THE TRAITOR?

Perhaps the most unexplored mystery in *Hellsing* is the identify of the traitorous member on the Knights of the Round Table. The Round Table was not explored in depth during the series, and only four members — including Integra — are named. This leaves a lot of leeway in determining the identity of the traitor. Indeed, the traitor may be one of the unnamed members of the Round Table.

Of the named members of the Knights of the Round Table, the easiest to rule out is Sir Integra Wingates Hellsing. She has no reason to fabricate such a scenario if all she wanted to do was lead the Hellsing Organisation to their doom, and she was present with Arucard in the final scene of the series, indicating that she was not tried and imprisoned for being a traitor.

Chief, the head of MI5, is a more likely suspect. While the Hellsing Organisation and MI5 worked together relatively closely, there were points of tension between the two. The death of Harry Anders is a wild card. While he seemed antagonistic towards Seras Victoria in early episodes, he was not above using her to help him obtain more information from the vampire Helena (see *Order 8: Kill House*). It's possible that he was believed to be too closely allied to Hellsing, and was thus killed so he was not able to interfere in MI5's potential betrayal of Hellsing. While this may explain Harry's murder, it does not explain why MI5 would want to betray the Hellsing Organisation.

In earlier episodes Sir Penwood — who is affiliated with the Ministry of Media Management — is very harsh towards Integra. He goes as far as to say that she is not as well suited to the job as her father was, and that he would never have been as brash and irresponsible as Penwood believes her to be. It is conceivable that Penwoods found the Hellsing Organisation's actions completely out of line, and chose to betray them instead of fighting them at the Round Table.

Sir Islands's relationship with the Hellsing Organisation is not delved into deeply. In earlier episodes, Islands appears to be in charge of the Round Table proceedings; perhaps he has the most seniority or is elected into that position. It is unclear to which organisation or organisations he belongs. Since he appears to have some measure of control over the Round Table proceedings, he seems to be in the best position to orchestrate a betrayal.

Without clear information on the six other members of the Knights of the Round Table, pinpointing the traitor is impossible. However, there is a wild card: Incognito. It's easily assumed that Incognito has the ability to read and control the minds of other beings, as he probably did with Boobanshee in *Order 9: Red Rose Vertigo*. If this is the case, Incognito may have influenced any of the Round Table members into betraying Hellsing (and along with Hellsing, the entire United Kingdom.) Such an act of treachery may seem implausible for anyone dedicated to the Queen and Country, but Incognito had no such allegiances and only wanted ultimate destruction.

There is also the slight possibility that Incognito's human master had a seat at the Round Table, but there is no evidence that this is true.

Palo Alto, USA Desert

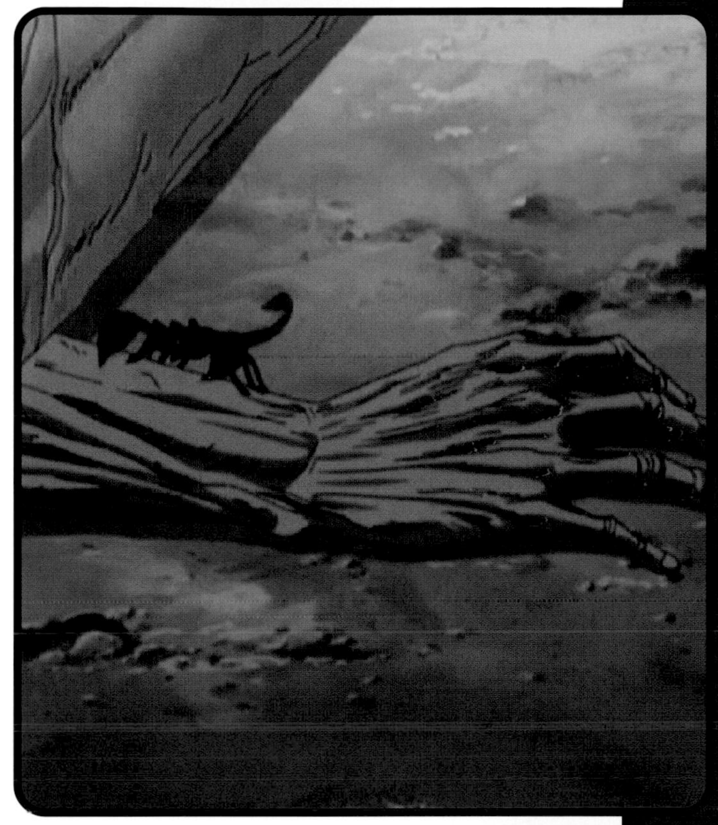

Early in *Order 8: Kill House*, an overturned car is shown in the Paolo Alto desert. A police helicopter flies overhead, identifying the dead person in the front seat as a suspect in a crime. The dead person's hand is briefly seen. It looks gaunt — perhaps vampiric or ghoulish in origin, or perhaps a result of the sweltering desert heat. A scorpion crawls over it, but for some reason, desert scavengers have not made a meal of the dead humanoid yet.

This event is not followed up on during the remainder of *Hellsing*, so viewers are left to speculate on what it could mean. Most likely it relates to the Freak chip vampires; the American authorities may be dealing with their own infestation, and this could be one of them. However, a simple car crash would likely not kill a chipped vampire. Another option is the victim is a ghoul — thus explaining the ugly appearance of his arm — but it's unclear why the ghoul would be the subject of a police manhunt. A third option is the man is somehow related to the manufacture or distribution of Freak chips, and that the American police are investigating them. This possibility is not mentioned anywhere else in the series, though, and since earlier in *Order 8: Kill House* a chip production facility was found in Hong Kong, this appears exceptionally unlikely.

Is Arucard Vlad the Impaler?

Two telltale signs that point to Arucard being Vlad the Impaler ... or perhaps a descendant of him. The first is the method that Arucard used to dispose of Incognito: impaling him on a long silver spike, and hanging him from the side of one of London Towers. This was the primary method of killing that Vlad the Impaler (Vlad Tepes) used during his reign as voivode (ruler) of Wallachia in the 1400s. Vlad Tepes is said to have killed tens of thousands of people during the three times he ruled Wallachia, many of them through inventive and torturous means.

The second is Arucard's physical appearance shortly after impaling Incognito. Still alive, Incognito says that what just happened was impossible, and asks Arucard who he really is. A lightning bolt illuminates half of Arucard's face, showing a face very similar to historical paintings of Vlad the Impaler.

These two events so close together are obviously not a coincidence, but they are the only two pieces of evidence pointing towards Arucard being linked to Vlad the Impaler (Aside from the amount of time that Arucard has spent on earth, which is unknown but presumed to be hundreds of years). Whether Arucard is Vlad the Impaler (and thus the *Hellsing* mythos has Vlad not dying in late 1476, but escaping somehow — given how his head was put on display on a stake after his death, not a likely option) or is merely some sort of descendant of his is unknown. Vlad had three sons from two different marriages, although we only know the names of two: Mihnea and Vlad. Mihnea briefly ruled Wallachia from 1508-1509, and was assassinated in 1510.

Another point of reference is Incognito's questioning of Paul Wilson, just before he is implanted with a Freak chip — his line of questioning is exceptionally similar to a quote attributed to Vlad Tepes, who once invited homeless people and vagrants in for a giant feast, and then burnt the building down around them, killing them all.

FREAK CHIPS: CYBERNETIC IMPLANTS

The latest scourge for the Hellsing Organisation comes not from the supernatural, but from black-market and illegal technology. Out of the same distribution markets as illegal pharmaceuticals and other illicit recreational substances comes the Freak chip, a device that promises power, ecstasy and immortal youth, all with a high from which you never come down.

The chips are rapidly spreading within the disaffected British populace, ranging from rebellious teenagers to tortured youths to the socially outcast. The hip and happening individuals in darker alternative scenes use the chips, such as the Valentine brothers. Although the users of the chip are not true vampires, just imitations, that limitation does not seem to faze those interested in acquiring one. This may be because they believe vampires to be a fictional creature of legend anyway. The chip's distributors use the mystique of the vampire, its sexual appeal, magical power and influence to make it appealing to the young, morbidly romantic, and disenfranchised.

Secondly, the chip itself looks like a modified sealed silicon circuit. There are dozens, perhaps one hundred thin flexible wires that extend from the edges of the chip in all directions. It's these wires that undoubtedly grant what mobility the chip is able to summon.

The probable function of the chip is to assume control of the nervous system and brain from the body's regular neural pathways. The wires act as detours for the signal, allowing the chip to take over the necessary autonomic body function and transfer signals from the brain to the spinal cord, as well as providing the necessary electrical power to transfer those signals.

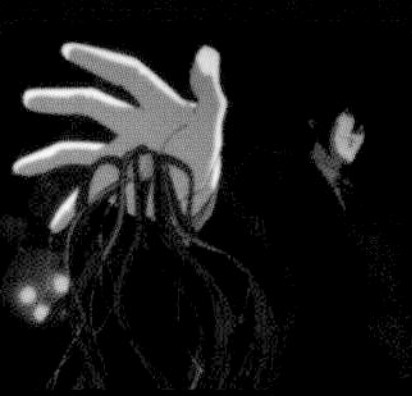

The result of the process is that the body changes, thus closing off any unnecessary body functions and the accompanying power drain, but keeping the brain and body functioning beyond the point of death. This would have the side effect of keeping the body from aging, though additional unknown processes are undoubtedly required to keep it from decaying. It is also unclear how the need for blood figures into a chipped vampire's physiology or how they are able to create ghouls.

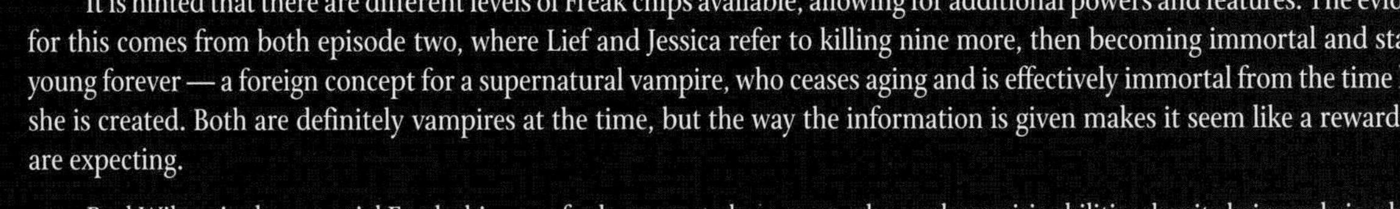

It is hinted that there are different levels of Freak chips available, allowing for additional powers and features. The evidence for this comes from both episode two, where Lief and Jessica refer to killing nine more, then becoming immortal and staying young forever — a foreign concept for a supernatural vampire, who ceases aging and is effectively immortal from the time he or she is created. Both are definitely vampires at the time, but the way the information is given makes it seem like a reward they are expecting.

Paul Wilson is also a special Freak chip user, for he seems to have more advanced vampiric abilities despite being only implanted with the chip within days of exhibiting the powers. He is able to influence Seras's dreams, and can turn both invisible and into werewolf form. These powers may be granted by the multiple Freak chips that burrow their way into his flesh, or Incognito may have somehow imbued him with or temporarily granted him additional powers.

There is also the fact that Jan and Luke Valentine in episodes five and six are by far the most powerful chipped vampires that the Hellsing Organisation has encountered. Luke's status is higher as the leader of the two, and he is the first chipped vampire we encounter who has anything resembling Arucard's powers. His super-speed is impressive, but it seems to be the only ability he has. He had never even considered the powers Arucard can manifest, the least of which was the degree of regeneration of which Arucard is capable. Even Andersong of Iscariot could boast a similar power, and his is also technologically based. That degree of "immortality" is beyond Luke's capability, suggesting that it is also a limitation of the chip he bears.

Despite the Valentine Brothers defeat during the raid on the Hellsing Mansion, the spread of Freak Chips continues throughout the British Isles and onto continental Europe. This attracts the attention of the Iscariot Organisation, so Enrico Maxwell and Father Renaldo visit Integra, telling her to get the Freak chip problem under control.

The opening scene to *Order 8: Kill House* reveals that at least some of the Freak chips are being manufactured in an unmarked building in Hong Kong. During a raid by Hong Kong authorities, the building and its contents — and perhaps even the people that work there — are destroyed so the police cannot gather evidence. This makes it safe to assume that the Freak chips are being manufactured in multiple places. Also, the building in which they were being constructed was not especially large, so the process must be refined and the equipment required compact and perhaps even portable. Later, Integra states that the chip designer was also killed in the explosion.

At a Knights of the Round Table meeting, technical details on the Freak chip are discussed. The technical name "Artificial Vampirisation Catalyst Semiconductors" is used once to describe them, but aside from the fancy name, the Knights have few pieces of solid intelligence about the chips. While they have a physical analysis of them, they still do not understand how it metamorphoses a human into a vampire. They believe that only a single chip is necessary to make someone undergo the transformation, and that the chip may work by activating information latent in human DNA. Integra clearly states at the same Knights of the Round Table meeting that she believes Hellsing's mission to keep the United Kingdom free of supernatural beasts also includes keeping it free of Freak chip-created vampires, and that Hellsing will search them out and destroy them. Seras's discussion with Helena reveals little about the Freak chips, except that Helena believes that they were somehow created with the help of another vampire.

It is also unsure whether biting bears any relevance to a vampire using the Freak chip in installing the chip in another user. Enrico bites his lover, Mick, but whether this was part of the process or simply a "love bite" was never discussed. It is unlikely that biting is helpful to the implant process, given the fragility of the chip and the imprecise nature of bite wounds.

The level of technical expertise and delicate construction of the chip indicate that it is a high-end product, requiring skilled technicians and expensive facilities to construct the items in any quantity. If the processes are the same as for any other microchip technology, then the tools and assembly procedures required would seem to make the construction of the implants almost impossible to hide. It may be that they are manufactured outside of the UK then shipped in. It could also be that the facility is disguised as a similar yet harmless type of manufacturing business and thus is able to continue production uninterrupted. Regardless, it remains to be seen if the law enforcement officials can stop the production and distribution of this product before any further attacks take place. This will only serve to heighten the tension between the Hellsing Organisation, the Vatican's Iscariot Organisation, and the Knights of the Round Table in the weeks and months to come.

VAMPIRES, SEX, AND DEATH

In the earliest legends, vampires were nothing but a source of horror for the people who told the tales. They were bloated demons, rising from the grave to prey upon the living. Children and the elderly were among their prime targets, although some varieties specialised in killing young men or maidens, such as the *rusalka*. Spirits who drank the blood of the living were often cited in mysterious or unexpected deaths occurring at night with no obvious causes. It served as a way for isolated societies to explain the unexplainable and make sense of it all.

Traditionally, vampires are hideous monsters who possess bloated bodies, long fingernails, dark red lips, and skin that carries the pallor of the grave. Their eyes are bloodshot and cruel, and the stench of death and rot is always with them. These can all be symptoms of bodily decomposition, of course, and were frequently mistaken as proof of vampirism by superstitious individuals anxious to protect their friends and families from a threat they could not otherwise identify.

In literature prior to the 1800s, the few vampires that are mentioned are never pleasant to see, instead being hideous monsters, the *nosferatu* with which Hollywood is familiar. It is not until the rise of gothic literature in the 19th century that an element of eroticism (and a pleasing appearance) enters into the legend of the vampire. In that age, science had finally come into its own. Many medical mysteries were finally explained. Art and culture were refined, and an abundance of wealth created a class that could afford to be bored and concentrate time and energy on amusements. In addition, the strict moral and social codes of the upper classes in Europe during the burgeoning Serasn age created a set of strong sexual and natural taboos, elements that naturally gave those topics a sensational appeal.

Polidori's vampire based on Lord Byron, Le Fanu's Carmilla, and even Varney the Vampire — all predecessors of Count Dracula — are attractive individuals whose appeal is undeniable to the other inhabitants of their fictional world. They are members of the upper class with somewhat unfortunate habits and enough compelling charisma to encourage others to overlook them. As damned creatures, they could display the sexual urges that upstanding members of the community could not, and thus give the reader a vicarious thrill without actually breaking social taboos. The drinking of blood, the ecstatic reaction it provokes, the strange compelling attraction and fascination, the raw uncivilised sensuality of the predator: all these forbidden and dangerously attractive elements drew the repressed culture of Serasn Europe as moths to a flame.

With *Dracula*, Stoker returned briefly to the unattractive model of the traditional vampire. Even he included a sexual element, however; the way Dracula chooses attractive and prized victims of the opposite sex for his own, the power he holds over their minds and bodies, the exchange of blood itself and the way he enters their rooms like a thief in the night. Dracula's actual appearance is easily overlooked — and has been in film, television and literature portrayals ever since.

In modern portrayals, the vampire is usually a handsome man who preys upon beautiful women who are typically single or in a loveless, distant marriage. Occasionally a female vampire will crop up, but typically they also prey upon women. It's perhaps evidence of male wish-fulfilment lurking behind the vampire's compelling image that modern female vampires who prey upon men are rare and typically created by women when traditionally, legends of evil female vampires who preyed upon men and children were far more common.

The vampire's second, more modern appeal is that of immortality. Among the traditional interpretation in strongly religious societies, it was assumed that the vampire's immortal life was a cursed, tortured existence. The soul became a vampire because it had been refused heaven and was one of the damned, and thus could never find peace. It was a terrible fate, and certainly not something to be desired.

Among modern interpretations in our more secular Western cultures, however, the vampire's immortality has little, if any drawbacks. The question of the afterlife for such creatures is far from settled, as the evidence of heaven and hell is no longer an assumed fact. To become a vampire is to never grow old, never become ill, and never die (unless someone takes it in mind to try and kill you). Add that fact to the sexual associations of the vampire discussed previously, and you have a powerfully attractive icon, the *puer*spirit made flesh, Peter Pan in a sexually mature adult form. It is little wonder that Rice's Lestat novels are so successful, or that the vampire continues to crop up in our culture when it badly needs escape from the messes mankind creates.

Hellsing uses these stereotypes as well, but not in the expected way. Arucard, far from being uncertain or uncaring regarding the state of the afterlife, knows exactly where the undead go: to hell. He is blunt, callous and mocking. He makes very little attempt to charm or be civilised, instead using his powers to remind all those around him of the predatory monster he is. Interestingly, he never uses his powers against any of his traditional prey — humans — unless specifically requested to do so. His bite is just as sweet to his victims as ever, but immediate death accompanies it. There is no foreplay involved, and no afterglow to enjoy, and he ensures that everyone knows it. Seras, the fledgling vampire, is even sexually harassed by Steadler. If she has compelling powers of sexual attraction due to her new condition, she certainly has not learned how to use them yet.

The villains, on the other hand, use sex as a lure constantly. From the nameless vampire at the manor house in the first episode posing as a prostitute to the priest at Cheddar who compliments Seras on the sweetness of her blood and boasts of the pleasure he'll offer her. From the teenage vampires who engage in violence and blood-induced orgies to the gay lovers with overactive romantic sensibilities. Sex is used as part of the sensual vampiric world, another taboo to be broken and another way to capture a quick bite to eat. Perhaps the ultimate expression of this in the first half of the series is the vampiric fetish club owned by Jan and Luke Valentine (their last name illustrating the point perfectly).

Immortality is shown as one of the primary reasons people seek out the Freak chip. Even Seras chooses to accept the embrace so as to avoid finality — a far cry from the virtuous figures in Serasn literature who eagerly accepted death, assured of the spotless state of their souls and their approaching eternal reward.

Hellsing, as with so many of the themes used in the series, turns these attractive qualities around to show us how empty they are, to fulfill the drawbacks of impossible promises. The protagonists are aware (or quickly learn) that getting your wish does not mean happily-ever-after, and that some wishes are better off not being granted at all. The search for the instant-gratification fast track may eventually lead to places you may wish you had never seen and, in the end, might get you killed at the hands of those who knew better in the first place.

Hellsing
Art Gallery

HELLSING TEASERS

END OF EPISODE #1
Subtitled

Man: No gal. No mecha. No eroticism.

Seras: Who says "gal" these days? Anyway, who are you?!

END OF EPISODE #2
Subtitled

Man: Tender and warm lief.

Lief: Humph.

Text: Plan well to use and return it...?

Seras: Plan well to use it. Hey, I'm asking who are you?!

END OF EPISODE #3
Subtitled

Man: Dancing priest. Impaled neck.

Seras: We just did that! This isn't a preview!

Man: Doing the "hot, hot, thing" among men! Insects crawl in Meguro Parasite Museum!

Seras: I like that place!

Man: R...really?!

END OF EPISODE #4
Dubbed

Man: Next time my true identity will be revealed.

Seras: That's enough. Our next episode ...

Man: Actually, I am ...

Seras: ... Brotherhood.

Man: Wait!

END OF EPISODE #5
Dubbed

Jan: I'm Jani.

Seras: Excuse me....

Luke: And I'm Luke.

Seras: Hey!

Jan and Luke: With the weather report.

Seras: Hang on....

Jan and Luke: Next week, *Hellsing* will have a rain of blood.

Seras: Again, being silly.

END OF EPISODE #6
Dubbed

Jan: It's Jani.

Luke: And Luke.

Jan and Luke: With the weather report.

Luke: Hey, didn't we lose?

Jan: We sure did. Hey bro', what's that weird thing eating your head.

Luke: Aaaaahhh. And you're on fire.

Hellsing Teasers

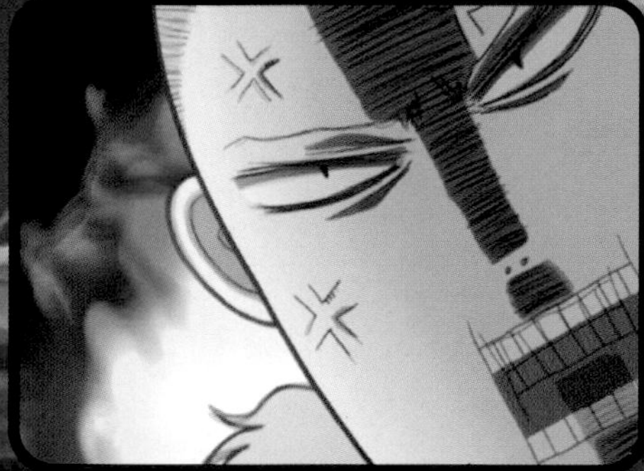

End of Episode #7
Subtitled

Enrico: Young miss, would you like to visit some museums with me?

Seras: What!?

Enrico: How about the library?

Seras: Huh?!

Man: Then how about my family jewel palace?!

Seras: We can't do that from the beginning...

Enrico: Such a difficult girl, right Father Renaldo?

End of Episode #8
Subtitled

Seras: OK, next week on Hellsing...

Man: Meaty bullet battle! Halconnen and Jackal spirit... and Walter goes shopping for the first time and Integra eats Fugu sashimi and drinks 3 beers...

Seras: I let you come back and you act like this?!

End of Episode #9
Subtitled

Man: I'm the fairy that lives inside your Halconnen Cannon.

Seras: Really?

Man: Actually, the trigger is here. Do you want to test shoot my Halconnen Cannon, too?

Seras: I won't use that anymore.

Man: Oh, it's a joke! Don't go away!

End of Episode #10
Subtitled

Walter: We exchange old newspapers, magazines and worn out clothes...

Seras: Tada! On the next expisode of Hellsing...

Walter: ... for tissue paper. We exchange...

Seras: Mr. Walter, what are you doing?

Walter: I thought this was the time for advertising?

Seras: Chiri-Gami (tissue paper) Walter... ?! (Shiri-Gami = Angel of Death) This is not a good preview.

End of Episode #11
Subtitled

Seras: Commander Fargason!

Peter: Victoria, fire to the right!

Seras: Yes!

Peter: Fire to the left!

Seras: Yes!

Peter: Fire towards tomorrow!

Seras: This really is an old man's gag.

End of Episode #12
Subtitled

Seras: The next episode of Hellsing is.... it'll be the final episode!

Seras: Will Hellsing and London finally have their peace.

Seras: Next episode, Order: 13 Hellfire!

Unknown: Fun and wonderful London!

Unknown: You finally did it, Police Girl!

Jesus Christ is in Heaven now
HELLSING ARMS WEAPON INDUSTRIALS CO.LTD.

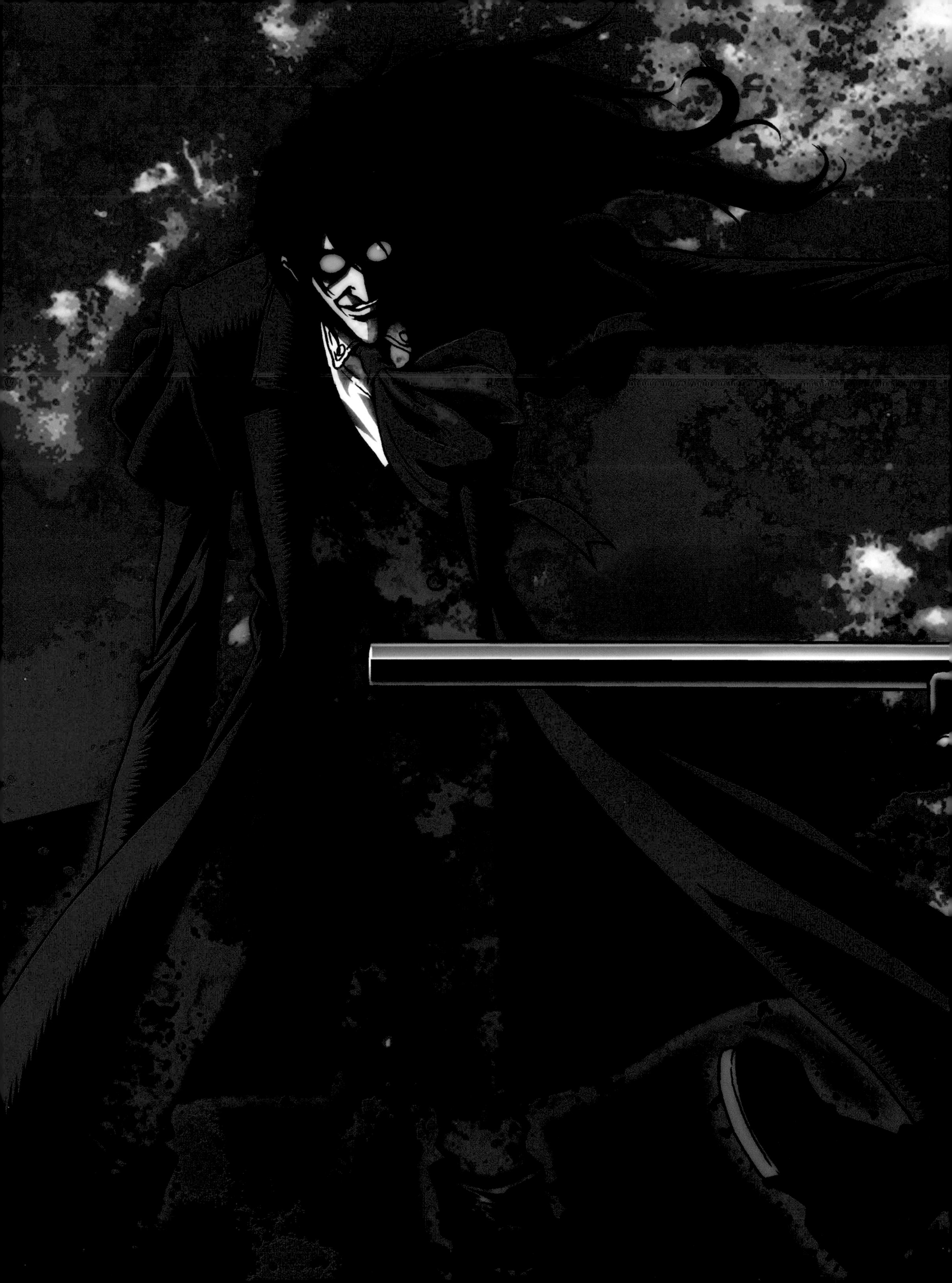

HELLSING ARMS WEAPON
INDUSTRIALS CO.LTD.

HELLSING
HELLS GATE ARRESTED
GOTT MIT UNS
AND SHINE HEAVEN NOW

HELLSING ARMS

Hellsing
In the name of God, impure souls of the living dead
shall be banished into eternal damnation. Amen.

決定稿
吸血牧師
2001.7 by T.MURATA
レイフとジェシカ
2001.7 by T.MURATA

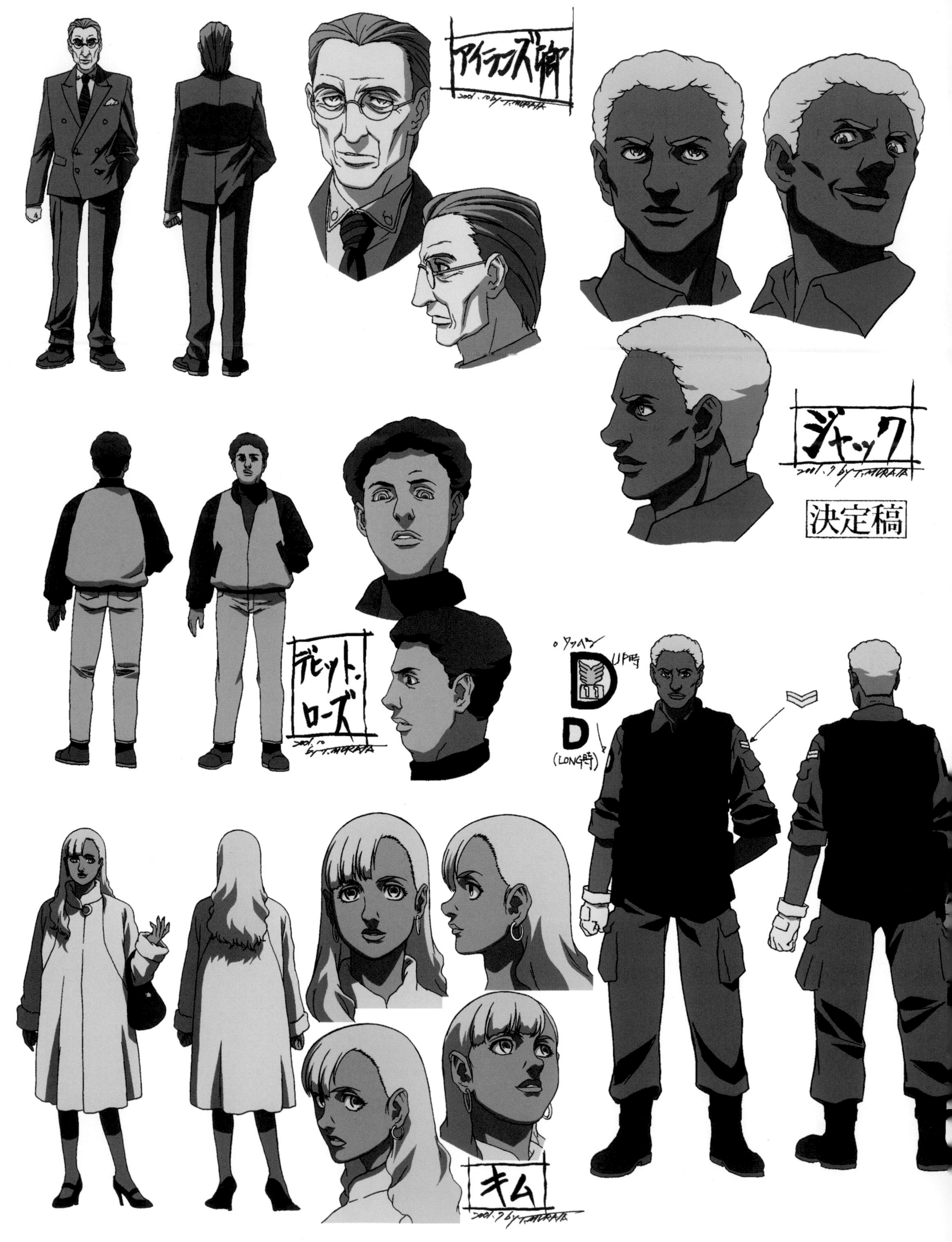

アイランズ卿
ジャック
決定稿
デビット・ローズ
キム

#9
インテグラの下僕

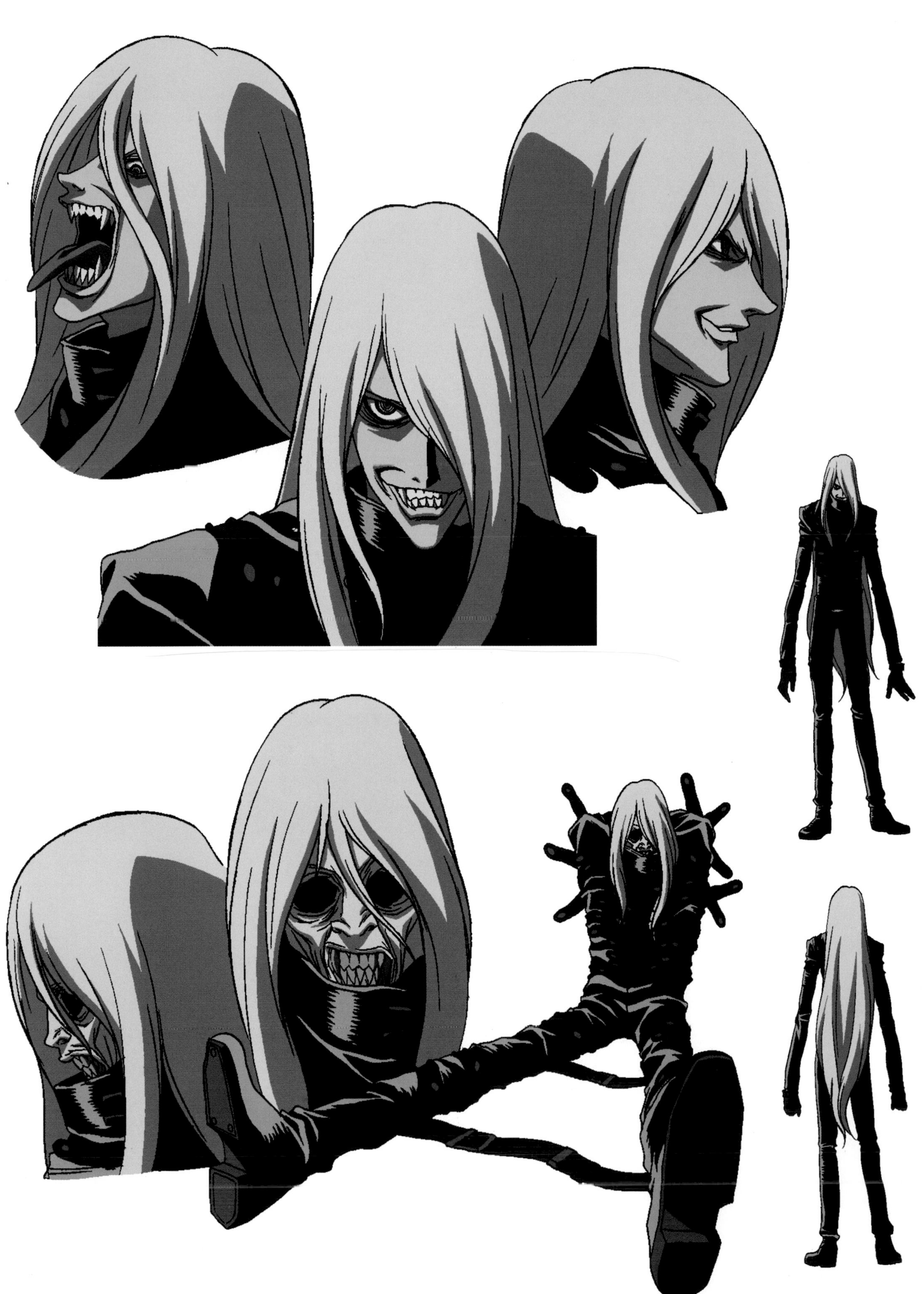

Hellsing Related Websites

Transport for London website, including information on the London Underground and other public transit within London. — http://www.tfl.gov.uk/tfl

The National Gallery, London — http://www.nationalgallery.org.uk

Official site of Historic Royal Palaces, including information about the Tower of London, Hampton Court Palace, Kensington Palace, Banqueting House, and Kew Palace — http://www.hrp.org.uk

Official MI5 site — http://www.mi5.gov.uk/

A user-maintained resource on the real-life history of the SAS — http://www.wikipedia.org/wiki/Special_Air_Service

The Official Web Site of the British Monarchy contains information on the members and history of the Royal Family, plus details on the Royal Residences — http://www.royal.gov.uk

A user-maintained resource on Vlad the Impaler — http://www.wikipedia.org/wiki/Vlad_Tepes

Vlad the Impaler resources compiled by Elizabeth Miller — http://www.ucs.mun.ca/~emiller/

General Anime Websites

Anime on DVD — a thorough site with anime release dates, reviews, licensing, and other anime related news — http://www.animeondvd.com/

Anime News Network — Anime and Manga news, convention reports, reviews, and more — http://www.animenewsnetwork.com/

GENEON ENTERTAINMENT (USA) INC. — formerly Pioneer Entertainment (USA) Inc., GENEON ENTERTAINMENT (USA) INC. is the North American distributor of *Hellsing* — http://www.geneonanimation.com/

Official Hellsing Site — Geneon's official site for Hellsing news and previews — http://hellsing.pioneeranimation.com/

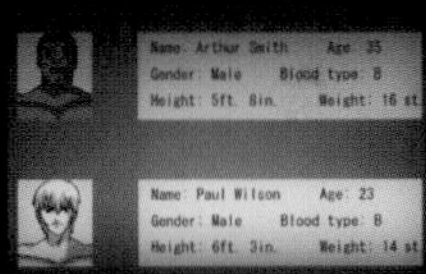

HELLSING d20 AND ROLE-PLAYING

Although most of the *Hellsing d20* provides resource and reference material for the series, some of the information in the following section is specifically included for those who wish to role-play in the world of Hellsing.

Guardians Of Order publishes a multi-genre Japanese anime role-playing game called Big Eyes, Small Mouth d20 Revised Edition (ISBN 1-894938-52-6). *BESM d20*, combined with the *PHB*, contains all the game rules, mechanics, and guidelines you need to establish an anime RPG campaign in any setting, genre, or time period. If you plan on hosting your game within the Hellsing setting, you may wish to use the game statistics provided for the series characters. Additionally, the reference lists, rules and suggestions for incorporating Hellsing elements into your game can provide vital insight into campaign construction. The Hellsing-specific material, in combination with the *BESM d20* rules, gives you everything you need to start role-playing right away.

If you are not familiar with that concept of table-top RPGs and would like to learn more, please visit our website at http://www.guardiansorder.com.

USING BESM d20 FOR A HELLSING CAMPAIGN

- The Own a Big Mecha special Attribute is disallowed, as are high-technology blaster weapons.
- Ability Scores above 16 in the *Hellsing* universe are not common.
- Powerful Weapons are acquired with the Special Attack Attribute.
- The suggested starting level is 6-8 with a Discretionary Point range of 38+1d10 (44) points. For vampires, the suggested starting level is 10.

Supernatural Creatures in Hellsing

The *Hellsing* universe is full of horrific supernatural monsters — undead that walk the night and seek sustenance from living human flesh. It is likely that characters in a *Hellsing* campaign will encounter these creatures, possibly losing companions to the scourge afflicting the countryside. Alternatively, the players may wish to play vampires, either of the true or chipped varieties in the course of the campaign.

The following section includes true and chipped vampire templates. Ghoul Stats are also given, but they are not recommended as player characters. If a character should be changed into a ghoul, it should become an NPC under the control of the GM and the player should generate a new character for the game. The series characters may vary slightly from the given templates.

Chipped Vampires

A chipped vampire is a human who has implanted a Freak chip. This chip effectively kills the body of the individual but sustains the mind and allows the user to continue to function beyond death. These individuals are similar to true vampires, though their abilities are limited and technologically based. It is thought that different levels of Freak chip are available, imparting varying degrees of power. The price for an upgrade, as well as the location and identity of the manufacturer/distributor, are still unknown. The template below lists the suggested Attributes and Defects of the most common version of the Freak chip.

Chipped Vampire Template

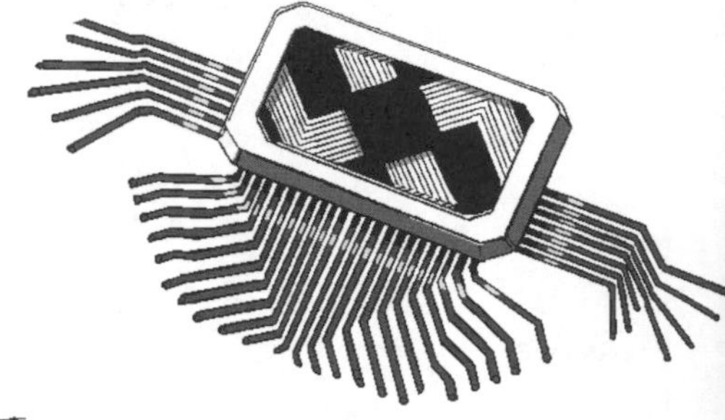

Cost: 50 Points

+2 Con +2 Cha

Attributes: Attack Combat Mastery 2, Contamination (Created Ghoul or Vampire) 5, Damn Healthy 1, Defence Combat Mastery 2, Feature (Longevity) 1, Magic (Vampiric) [Mind Control (Created Ghouls) 5, Mind Control (Fearful Humans) 1, Regeneration 4] 4, Natural Weapons (Fangs) 1, Special Attack (Vampiric Bite) [1d8 , Incapacitating, Drain Soul, Vampiric, Low Penetration, Melee] 4

Defects: Bane (Silver) 1, Bane (Sunlight) 2, Marked (Red eyes, fangs) 1, Vampirism 1, Vulnerability (Fire) 1, Vulnerability (Silver) 1

Chipped Super Vampires

This character is identical to a Chipped Vampire, but has additional powers — either granted by the implantation of multiple Freak chips, or granted to them by a Master Vampire who oversees the chip implantation.

Chipped Super Vampire Template

Cost: 60 Points

+2 Con +2 Cha

Attributes: Attack Combat Mastery 2, Contamination (Created Ghoul or Vampire) 5, Damn Healthy 2, Defence Combat Mastery 2, Feature (Longevity) 1, Magic (Vampiric): [Alternate Form (Werewolf) 1, Insubstantial 4, Mind Control (Created Ghouls) 5, Mind Control (Fearful Humans) 1, Regeneration 4] 7, Natural Weapons (Fangs) 1, Special Attack (Vampiric Bite) [1d8, Incapacitating, Drain Soul (Wisdom), Vampiric, Low Penetration, Melee] 4

Defects: Bane (Silver) 1, Bane (Sunlight) 2, Marked (Red eyes, fangs) 1, Owned by a Master Vampire 2, Vampirism 2, Vulnerability (Fire) 1, Vulnerability (Silver) 1, Wanted 2

Werewolf Form: Features (Fur) 1, Natural Weapons (Fangs, claws) 2, Speed 1

TRUE VAMPIRES

True vampires are created by the bite of a true supernatural vampire. They owe no allegiance to technology, instead being solely paranormal creatures. A newly created true vampire may be weaker than a chipped vampire, but his or her powers will grow as the vampire gains experience. Most of the true vampire's later powers are available as Attributes: Swarm, Heightened Senses, Invisibility, etc.The template below is for a newly created true vampire. A vampire is subject to the will of the vampire who created him or her, and must attempt to obey any orders given by the master vampire.

TRUE VAMPIRE TEMPLATE

COST: 60 POINTS

+2 Con +2 Cha

Attributes: Attack Combat Mastery 3, Contamination (Created Ghoul or Vampire) 5, Damn Healthy 1, Defence Combat Mastery 3, Feature (Longevity) 1, Heightened Senses (Vision) 1, Magic (Vampiric) [Mind Control (Created Ghouls) 5, Mind Control (Fearful Humans) 1, Regeneration 4] 4, Natural Weapons (Fangs) 1, Special Attack (Vampiric Bite) [1d8, Incapacitating, Drain Soul (Wisdom), Vampiric, Low Penetration, Melee] 4, Special Attack (Conversion Bite) [1d8, Incapacitating, Vampiric, Low Penetration, Melee] 1, Super Strength 1

Defects: Bane (Silver) 1, Bane (Sunlight) 2, Marked (Red eyes, fangs) 1, Owned by a Master Vampire 2, Vampirism 2, Vulnerability (Blessed Weapons) 1, Vulnerability (Fire) 1, Vulnerability (Silver) 1

VAMPIRE WEAPON ATTACKS

VAMPIRIC BITE

All vampires gain the Vampiric Bite Weapon Attack Attribute (Damage 1d8, Incapacitate, Drain Soul (Wisdom), Vampiric, Low Penetration, Melee). The target of a Vampiric Bite is overwhelmed with pleasurable feelings, rendering the victim incapacitated. A victim whose Wisdom is drained to zero is turned into a ghoul (see below) and immediately turned over to the GM as an NPC. The Wisdom Points gained can be used to increase the vampire's Wisdom above her normal maximum value temporarily.

VAMPIRIC CONVERSION

A true vampire renders the victim of a Vampiric Conversion attack incapacitated as well (Damage 1d8, Incapacitating, Vampiric, Low Penetration, Melee). The victim is turned into a true vampire (through the Contamination Attribute) when his or her Hit Points are reduced to zero by this attack.

GHOULS

Ghouls are created when a vampire kills a victim using the Vampiric Bite attack. They are not appropriate for use as characters because they have no free will and are under the complete control of the vampire who created them. A character who becomes a ghoul should be surrendered to the GM to be played as an NPC.

Ghouls have the appearance of a corpse, with grey sagging skin, sunken blank eyes and jagged grey teeth. They are clumsy and shamble when they walk. Their only motivation other than the will of their master is to consume human flesh, which is their only source of nourishment. Once a character has become a ghoul, it cannot be made human again. When a ghoul is killed, its body turns immediately into dust.

GHOUL TEMPLATE

17 Discretionary Points for Attributes

Ghoul, HD 1d8+1, Hit Points 7, Energy Points 0, Initiative +0, Speed 24ft, AC 0, Base Attack +0, Fort +1, Ref +0, Will –5, Str 11 (0), Dex 8 (-1), Con 12 (+1), Int 2 (-4), Wis 1 (-5), Cha 0 (-5)

Attack +0 melee (1d4, Claws)

Attributes: Damn Healthy! 1, Features (Longevity) 1, Natural Weapons (Claws, fangs) 2

Defects: Marked 2, Owned by Master Vampire 2, Unskilled 1

Arucard

Adventurer 30/Martial Artist 4, Discretionary Points 44, Medium-sized True Vampire, HD 30d4+120 plus 4d10+16, Hit Points 276, Energy Points 133, Initiative +8, Speed 57ft., AC 7 (DCM +3, Dex +4), Base Attack +22/+17/+12/+7, Fort +15, Ref +18, Will +17, Str 20 (+5), Dex 18 (+4), Con 18 (+4), Int 14 (+2), Wis 16 (+3), Cha 18 (+4)

Attacks: +34, +34, +34, +29, +24, +19 melee (1d8+7, *Unarmed Strike*) or +31, +31, +31, +26, +21, +16 melee (1d8+7, Incapacitating, Drain Soul (Wisdom), Vampiric, Low Penetration, *Vampiric Bite*), or +22, +22, +22, +17, +12, +7 ranged (2d8, Concealable, Penetrating (Armour), Short Range, Burning, *13mm Jackal*), or +22, +22, +22, +17, +12, +7 ranged (2d8, Concealable, Penetrating (Armour), Short Range, *.454 Casull*)

Attributes: Attack Combat Mastery 3, Aura of Command 2, Contamination (Ghoul or Vampire) 5, Damn Healthy! 2, Defence Combat Mastery 3, Energy Bonus 4, Extra Attacks 2, Feature (Longevity) 1, Heightened Awareness 2, Heightened Senses (Vision) 1, Magic (Vampiric) 13 [Alternate Form (Wolf Head) 2, Flight (Skimmer) 1, Insubstantial 4, Invisibility 1, Mind Control (Humans, Created Vampires and Ghouls) 5, Pocket Dimension (Netherworld) 5, Regeneration 5, Reincarnation 6, Swarm (Bats) 1, Swarm (Insects) 1, Telekinesis 3, Telepathy 3], Massive Damage (Unarmed) 2, Natural Weapons (Fangs) 1, Organisational Ties (Hellsing) 4, Special Attack (Vampiric Bite) 4, Special Attack (Conversion Bite) 3, Special Attack (13mm Jackal) 4, Special Attack (Demonic Form) 4, Special Attack (Hell's Gate Arrested) 4, Special Attack (.454 Casull) 3, Special Movement (Untrackable, Wall Crawling) 2, Super Strength 1

Skills: Bluff (Misleading Body Language) 15, Hide (Skulking) 15, Intimidation (Street) 21, Knowledge: Arcane (Magic) 18, Knowledge: Occult (Spirits) 18, Move Silently (Soft Step) 26, Sense Motive (Mannerisms) 18, Unarmed Attack (Strikes) 9, Unarmed Defence (Strikes) 9, Wilderness Tracking (Urban) 29

Feats: Accuracy, Brawl, Dodge, Frightful Presence, Improved Brawl, Improved Initiative, Judge Opponent, One Bullet Left, Point Blank Shot, Rapid Shot, Steady Hand

Defects: Bane (Silver) 1, Bane (Sunlight) 3, Easily Distracted (Worthy Challenges) 1, Marked (Red eyes, fangs) 1, Nemesis (Andersong) 1, Nemesis (Incognito) 2, Owned by the Hellsing Organisation 2, Restriction (Attacking Integra Targets) 2, Unique (Only Level 3 human Mind Control) 2, Vampirism 2, Vulnerability (Blessed weapons) 1, Vulnerability (Fire) 1, Vulnerability (Silver) 1

Alternate Form (Wolf Head)

Attributes: Elasticity 2, Extra Attack 1, Massive Damage (Bite) 4

Background

Magic

While Arucard is a god-like being, he bears some form of restriction as part of his service to the Hellsing Organization. These take the form of a control art restriction" and a "power restriction." He refers to them as "systems," but they don't appear to be technological in nature. It is uncertain whether they are limitations or simply a method of classifying his powers.

Before he uses many of his powers, he speaks a code phrase regarding the restriction systems mentioned above. It is unclear whether this phrase actually unlocks the power or whether it is merely spoken to keep an unseen person informed of his actions. It is possible that these statements, often uttered along with status checks regarding his assignment, are being telepathically communicated to Integra at the same time. It is left to the GM to decide what limits or constraints if any have been placed on Arucard.

Other Game Notes

Explanations regarding some of Arucard's magical abilities are as follows:

- Dimensional Portal to the Netherworld — Arucard can open a portal to a dark mirror of the regular world. It requires a level 5 release of Arucard's control art restriction system.
- Insect Swarm — Arucard can transform himself into a swarm of crawling insects, such as centipedes. It requires a level 3 release of Arucard's control art restriction system.

Attack Restriction

Arucard may only attack the targets Integra assigns to him. He is seemingly forbidden to attack anyone who is not undead except in self-defense, with the possible exception of the Iscariot Organization's Paladin Alexander Andersong. He may not feed off humans, with the exception of the reporter, Kim.

Owned by the Hellsing Organization

Arucard refers to himself as being "in servitude" to humans, and the Hellsing Organization in particular. He obeys the orders of Integra Hellsing even though he is far more powerful than she, and tolerates being upbraided by her on occasion. The reason for this servitude is not revealed in the first half of the series, but it is intimated that Arucard has served the Hellsing family since Abraham Von Hellsing, Integra's great-grandfather and creator of the Hellsing Foundation.

Nemesis

Arucard's Nemesis is Paladin Alexander Andersong of the Iscariot Organization.

Weapon Attacks

.454 Casull pistol with exploding silver rounds (blessed)

13 mm Jackal pistol with silver mercury charged rounds (blessed)

Demonic Form — Damage 3d8, Aura, No Regeneration, Melee. This attack allows Arucard to transform into a shapeless black form covered in red eyes and fanged mouths. In order to take this form, Arucard releases all levels of both power and art restrictions. It is his most powerful attack, and requires special permissions to activate (Cromwell approval).

Hell's Gate Arrested — Damage 4d8, Linked (Dimensional Portal), No Damage. This attack facilitates the transport of individuals to the Netherworld.

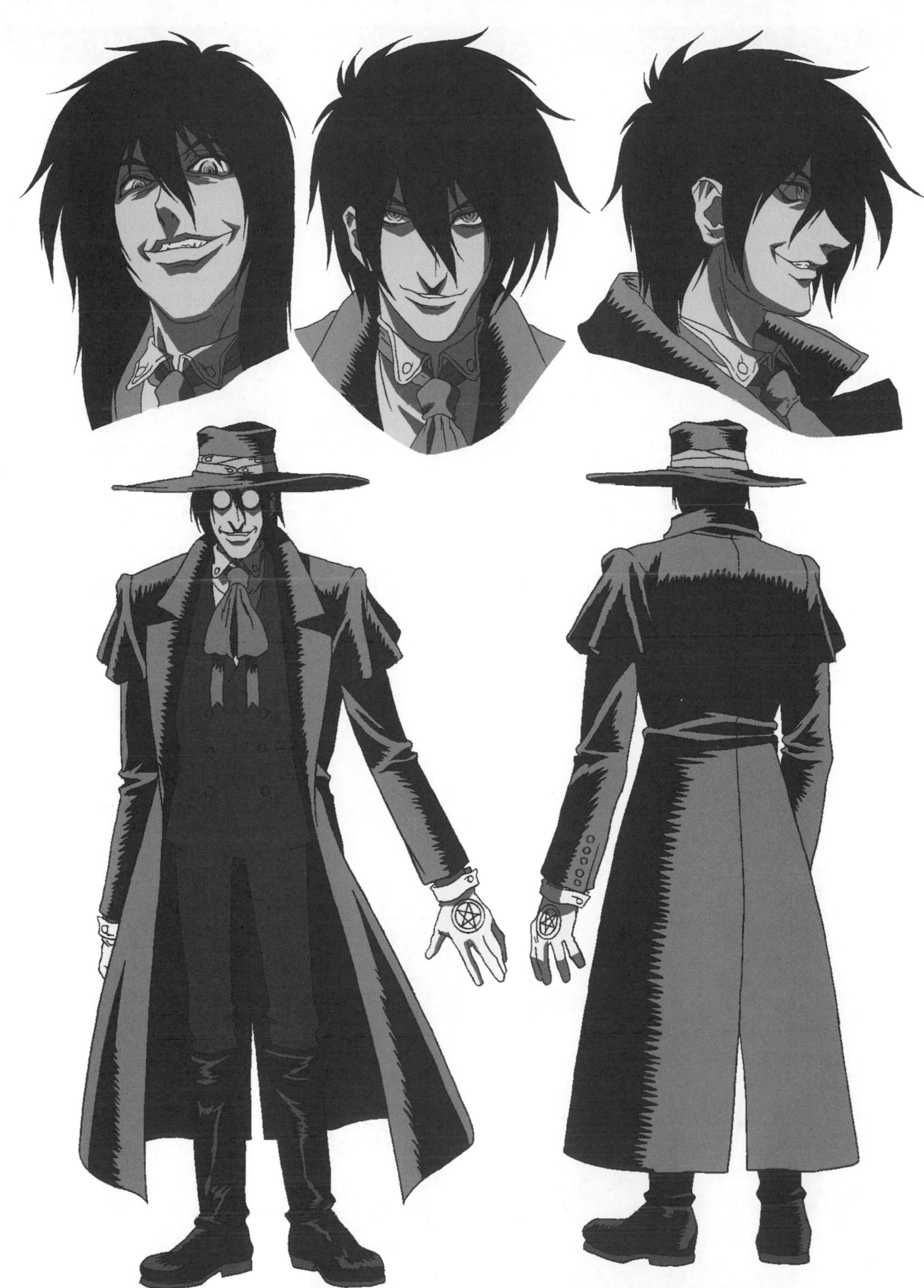

Incognito

Adventurer 28/Martial Artist 3, Discretionary Points 44, Medium-sized True Vampire, HD 28d4+112 plus 3d10+12, Hit Points 260, Energy Points 128, Initiative +8, Speed 54ft., AC 7 (DCM +3, Dex +4), Base Attack +20/+15/+10/+5, Fort +14, Ref +16, Will +15, Str 21 (+5), Dex 18 (+4), Con 19 (+4), Int 14 (+2), Wis 16 (+3), Cha 18 (+4)

Attacks: +31, +31, +26, +21, +16 melee (1d8+7, Unarmed Strike) or +28, +28, +23, +18, +13 melee (1d8+7, Incapacitating, Drain Soul, Vampiric, Low Penetration, *Vampiric Bite*), or +24 ranged (3d8, Area Effect, Burning, Indirect, Long Range, Unique Ability (Continuous Strike), Inaccurate, Slow, *Energy Beam*) or +20, +20, +15, +10, +5 ranged (3d8, Auto-fire, Low Penetration, *Arms Corps 40mm*) or +20, +20, +15, +10, +5 (1d8, Area Effect, Incapacitating, No Damage, *Freezing Tomb*)

Attributes: Attack Combat Mastery 3, Contamination (Ghoul or Vampire) 5, Damn Healthy! 3, Defence Combat Mastery 3, Energy Bonus 4, Extra Attacks 1, Feature (Longevity) 1, Heightened Awareness 1, Heightened Senses (Vision) 1, Magic (Vampiric) 13 [Flight (Skimmer) 1, Insubstantial 4, Invisibility 1, Mind Control (Humans, Created Vampires and Ghouls) 5, Regeneration 5, Reincarnation 6, Telekinesis 3, Telepathy 3, Teleportation 6], Massive Damage (Unarmed) 2, Natural Weapons (Fangs) 1, Special Attack (Vampiric Bite) 4, Special Attack (Conversion Bite) 3, Special Attack (Energy Beam) 6, Special Attack (Arms Corps 40mm) 3, Special Attack (Freezing Tomb) 1, Super Strength 1

Skills: Intimidation (Street) 19, Knowledge: Arcane (Magic) 12, Knowledge: Occult (Spirits) 12, Sense Motive (Mannerisms) 12, Special Ranged Attack (Energy Beam) 8, Survival (Forest) 22, Unarmed Attack (Strikes) 8, Unarmed Defence (Strikes) 8, Wilderness Tracking (Forest) 25

Feats: Accuracy, Brawl, Dodge, Frightful Presence, Improved Brawl, Improved Initiative, Steady Hand

Defects: Bane (Silver) 1, Bane (Sunlight) 2, Marked (Red eyes, fangs, grey skin and genderless) 2, Nemesis (Hellsing Organisation) 2, Vampirism 2, Vulnerability (Blessed weapons) 1, Vulnerability (Fire) 1, Vulnerability (Silver) 1

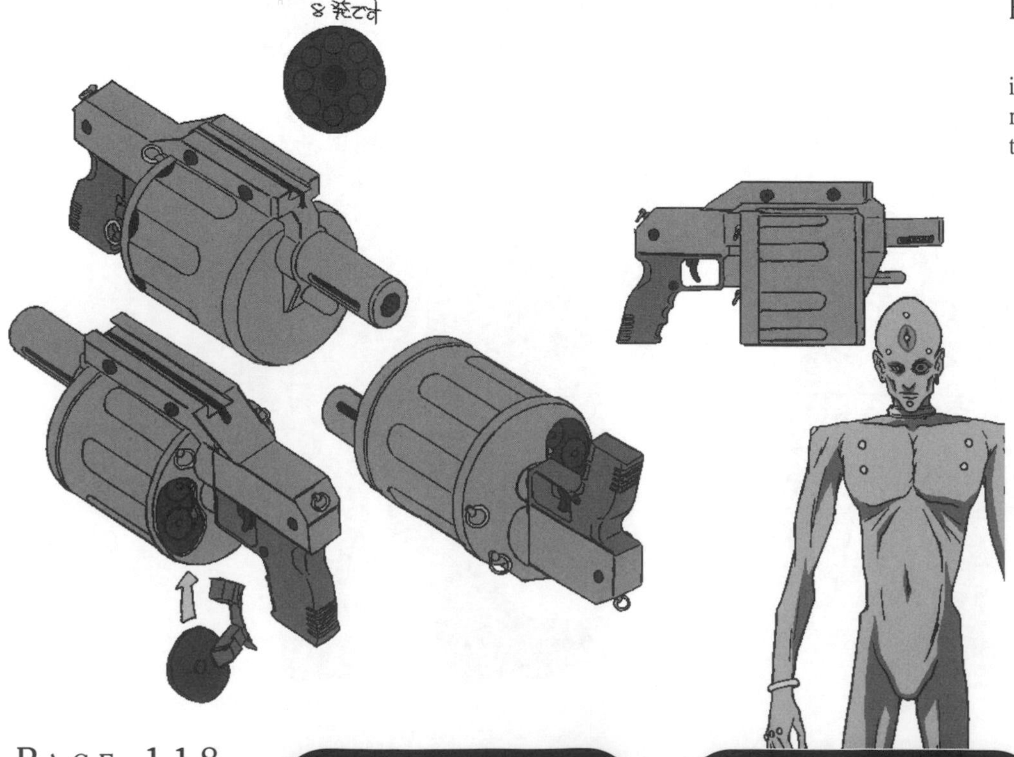

Other Game Notes

Magic

Incognito does not seem to have any tethers on his magical abilities. He does have ritualistic tendencies, but they seem to be a matter of posturing rather than necessity.

Nemesis (Hellsing Organisation)

Incognito is new to the British Isles, but his vampiric presence is enough to make him an enemy of Hellsing. They have no choice but to destroy him before he devastates London.

Weapon Attacks

ArmsCorps 40mm MGM with flechette rounds.

The ArmsCorps 40mm MGM is a short-barrelled firearm with a revolving drum. It could be loaded with regular ammunition, changing the values to Damage 3d8, Auto-Fire.

Energy Beam

Incognito's Energy Beam attack can manifest in several forms. In one instance he uses it to sound a "bouncing" beam of blue light across the London landscape; in another he sends a cutting "sound wave" in all directions. The bouncing beam can continue causing damage every three to five rounds (representing the time it takes to "jump" and attack) at the GM's discretion.

Freezing Tomb

Multiple targets are temporarily imprisoned in blocks of ice with Freezing Tomb. The caster can release them from the blocks at any time, causing the ice to shatter and melt instantly.

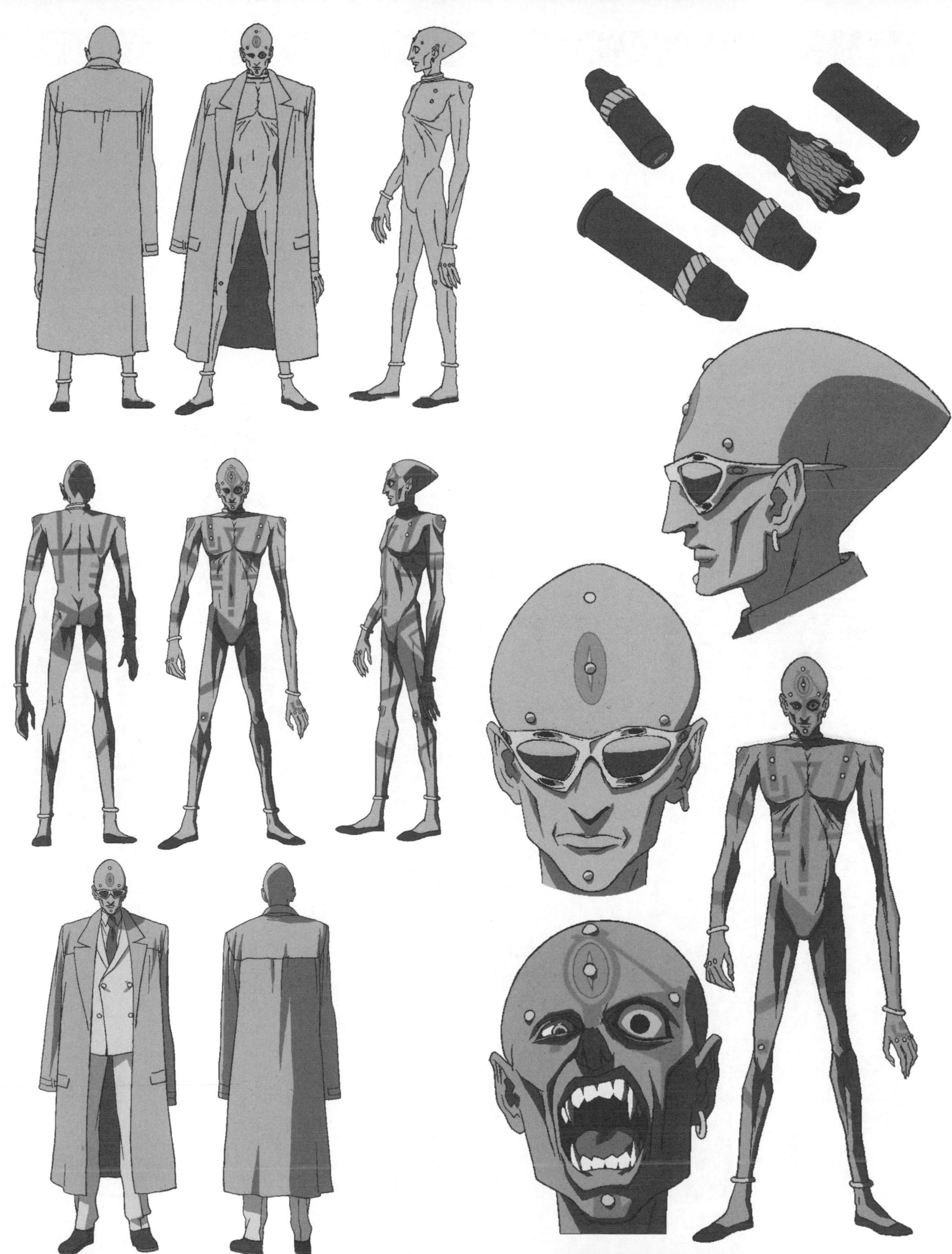

Sir Integra Wingates Hellsing

Adventurer 5/Gun Bunny 2, Discretionary Points 44, Medium-sized Human, HD 5d4 plus 2d8, Hit Points 39, Energy Points 14, Initiative +4, Speed 33ft., AC 0, Base Attack +4, Fort +1, Ref +4, Will +6, Str 10 (0), Dex 11 (0), Con 10 (0), Int 18 (+4), Wis 17 (+3), Cha 18 (+4)

Attacks: +10 ranged (1d8+1, Concealable, Low Penetration, Burning, Short Range, *Heavy Pistol*)

Attributes: Art of Distraction 3, Aura of Command 3, Damn Healthy! 2, Divine Relationship 1, Heightened Awareness 1, Highly Skilled 2, Organisational Ties (Hellsing) 5, Personal Gear (Pistol) 1

Skills: Bluff (Misdirection) 6, Diplomacy (Negotiation) 7, Gather Information (Contacts) 6, Gun Combat (Pistol) 5, Intimidation (Political) 9, Knowledge: Business (Executive) 8, Knowledge: Law (British Criminal Law) 7, Knowledge: Military Sciences (Intelligence Analysis) 8, Knowledge: Police Sciences (Forensics) 7, Knowledge: Occultism (Witchcraft) 8, Sense Motive (Speech) 7

Feats: Accuracy, Far Shot, Improved Initiative, Iron Will, Point Blank Shot

Defects: Nemesis (Traitor from Knights of the Round Table) 1, Red Tape 1

Other Game Notes

Organizational Ties

Integra is the head of the Hellsing Organization and works in concert with the other members of the Knights of the Round Table, a group of high-ranking government individuals including the head of MI-5 (the British intelligence agency).

Personal Gear

Integra carries an automatic pistol with mercury ignition rounds (blessed).

WALTHER
Car. Walther-Waffenfabrik Ulm/Do.
PPK Cal. 9mm kurz W.Germany
HELLSING
WALTER
PPK

SERAS VICTORIA

Adventurer 13/Gun Bunny 2, Discretionary Points 44, Medium-sized True Vampire, HD 13d4+26 plus 2d8+4, Hit Points 105, Energy Points 22, Initiative +7, Speed 48ft., AC 6 (DCM +3, Dex +3), Base Attack +11/+6/+1, Fort +7, Ref +10, Will +6, Str 20 (+5), Dex 16 (+3), Con 15 (+2), Int 11 (0), Wis 12 (+1), Cha 14 (+2)

Attacks: +12, +7, +2 melee (1d6+5, *Unarmed Strike*) or +11, +6, +1 melee (1d8+5, Incapacitating, Drain Soul, Vampiric, Low Penetration, *Vampiric Bite*) or +19, +14, +9 ranged (1d8+2, Auto-fire, Penetrating (Armour), *Barret Light Rifle*) or +11 (3d8, Penetrating (Armour), Static, Limited Shots x3, *30mm Halconnen*)

Attributes: Attack Combat Mastery 3, Contamination (Ghoul or Vampire) 5, Damn Healthy! 3, Defence Combat Mastery 3, Divine Relationship 1, Feature (Longevity) 1, Heightened Awareness 1, Heightened Senses (Vision) 1, Magic (Vampiric) 5 [Mind Control (Created Ghouls) 5, Mind Control (Fearful Humans) 1, Regeneration 4], Natural Weapons (Fangs) 1, Organisational Ties (Hellsing) 3, Special Attack (Vampiric Bite) 4, Special Attack (Conversion Bite) 3, Special Attack (30mm Halconnen) 1, Super Strength 1

Skills: Gun Combat (Rifle) 7, Knowledge: Law (British Criminal Law) 9, Knowledge: Military Sciences (Tactics) 9, Knowledge: Police Sciences (Criminology) 15, Ranged Defence (Personal) 6

Feats: Accuracy, Brawl, Improved Initiative, Steady Hand

Defects: Bane (Silver) 1, Bane (Sunlight) 2, Marked (Red eyes, fangs) 1, Owned by Unknown Master Vampire 2, Restriction (Attack only monsters) 1, Vampirism 2, Vulnerability (Blessed weapons) 1, Vulnerability (Fire) 1, Vulnerability (Silver) 1

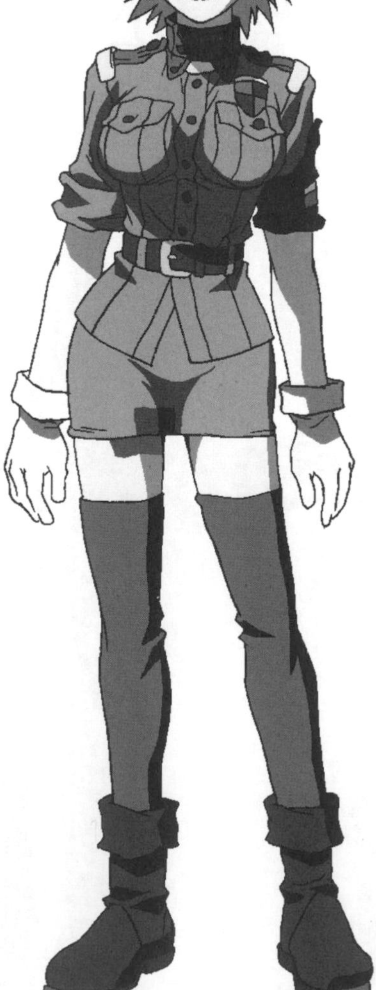

OTHER GAME NOTES

ATTACK RESTRICTION

Seras is very hesitant to kill anything or anyone that isn't obviously a monster. She finds it difficult to fire on anyone who might be an innocent, even under direct orders. She is overcoming this restriction, but any time she is forced to fire, she is wracked by feelings of horror and guilt for days thereafter.

OWNED BY ARUCARD

Seras is largely under the command of Arucard. While she still has free will in most matters, she acknowledges his control and calls him Master. She attempts to follow his orders, but by a struggle of will she can disobey him if she feels she must.

PERSONAL GEAR

Seras is assigned a rifle in Episode 2. This rifle is a powerful weapon, likely based upon the Barret Light .50 rifle. The Barret light 0.50 fires the same ammunition as the large fifty-calibre machine gun.

WEAPON ATTACKS

Seras also uses a 30mm Halconnen, which fires both depleted uranium rounds and explosive incendiary rounds used in armoured vehicular weaponry. Depleted uranium rounds add Spreading x2 to the weapon — up to 6 targets (targets must be in a line). Explosive rounds add Area Effect.

HELLSING
セラスのライフル

WALTER DDOLLNEAZZ

Adventurer 12, Discretionary Points 44, Medium-sized Human, HD 12d4+24, Hit Points 60, Energy Points 21, Initiative +2, Speed 45ft., AC 5 (DCM +3, Dex +2), Base Attack +9/+4, Fort +6, Ref +6, Will +7, Str 14 (+2), Dex 15 (+2), Con 14 (+2), Int 16 (+3), Wis 16 (+3), Cha 17 (+3)

Attacks: +21, +21, +21, +16 melee (2d8+2, Accurate, Area Effect, Concealable, Flexible, *Finger Monowire Garrotte*)

Attributes: Aura of Command 1, Attack Combat Mastery 3, Defence Combat Mastery 3, Divine Relationship 1, Extra Attacks 2, Heightened Awareness 2, Organisational Ties (Hellsing) 4, Special Attack (Finger Monowire Garrotte) 4

Skills: Computer Use (Networks) 13, Hide (Concealment) 15, Knowledge: Occultism (Witchcraft) 11, Knowledge: Social Sciences (Psychology) 9, Melee Attack (Monowire Gloves) 7, Move Silently (Soft Step) 15

Feats: Accuracy, Judge Opponent, Steady Hand, Weapons Encyclopaedia

OTHER GAME NOTES

WEAPON ATTACK

Finger Monowire Garrotte — Walter extends thin monowires from his gloves, using them to decapitate or otherwise maim his opponents.

Paladin Alexander Andersong

Adventurer 12/Samurai 5, Discretionary Points 44, Medium-sized Human, HD 12d4+24 plus 5d8+10, Hit Points 115, Energy Points 28, Initiative +6, Speed 42ft., AC 5 (DCM +3, Dex +2) Base Attack 14/+9/+4, Fort +10, Ref +7, Will +8, Str 14 (+2), Dex 14 (+2), Con 16 (+3), Int 16 (+3), Wis 16 (+3), Cha 19 (+4)

Attacks: +23, +23, +23, +23, +18, +13 melee (1d8+2, *Blessed Sword*)

Attributes: Attack Combat Mastery 3, Aura of Command 2, Damn Healthy! 1, Defence Combat Mastery 3, Divine Relationship 1, Extra Attacks 3, Heightened Awareness 2, Organisational Ties (Iscariot) 3, Personal Gear (Blessed Swords) 1, Regeneration 5, Unique Attribute (Purifying Ward) 2

Skills: Gather Information (Contacts) 7, Hide (Concealment) 9, Intimidation (Street) 16, Investigate (Government) 7, Knowledge: Occultism (Witchcraft) 15, Knowledge: Social Sciences (Theology) 15, Melee Attack (Sword) 8, Melee Defence (Sword) 8, Move Silently (Soft Step) 16, Wilderness Tracking (Urban) 7

Feats: Accuracy, Ambidexterity, Improved Initiative, Judge Opponent, Two Weapon Fighting

Defects: Incomplete Training (Speed level 1) 2, Nemesis (Alucard) 1, Restriction (May only attack Iscariot targets) 1, Special Requirement (Prayer) 1

Other Game Notes

Organizational Ties

Andersong is a Catholic priest and a member of the Iscariot Organization — a division devoted to combating and destroying the undead wherever they are found. He holds the rank of Paladin. He is also connected to the Vatican's secret bureau, Section Thirteen.

Personal Gear

Andersong attacks using blessed single-edged short swords — Damage 1d8+2, Accurate, Affects Incorporeal, Concealable, Melee. Although primarily melee weapons, he can throw them a few metres when necessary.

Special Requirement

Before any combat action, Andersong gives a brief and sometimes bloodthirsty prayer for the soul of the person he's about to attack. It remains to be seen whether this is merely habit for him or a necessary part of his regimen.

Unique Attribute

Alexander Andersong is a Catholic priest who specializes in dealing with the undead. To help him in his quest against the forces of darkness, he has perfected a method of warding an area against vampiric powers, blocking their use. In order to use the purifying ward, Andersong must secure blessed pieces of paper inscribed with arcane symbols around the area to be affected (requires one combat action). The ward is in effect for as long as the papers remain in place and does not need to be maintained.

Purifying Ward — Special Attack: Area Effect, Unique Ability (block vampiric Magical Powers), No Damage, Focus — arcane papers, 8 Energy Points to invoke.

Attack Restriction

Andersong is not supposed to attack anyone other than his assigned target. This does not always stop him, especially if he sees the chance to rid the world of either additional undead or a representative of the Hellsing Organization. He is answerable for his actions, however, and must make a full accounting to his superior upon returning home.

Nemesis

Andersong gains Arucard as a Nemesis following their encounter in Episode 3. While they duel to a standstill in Episode 7, it is clear that Arucard would happily kill the priest when next they meet. When Arucard receives the 13mm Jackal, Seras asks if the gun could kill Andersong, to which Arucard replies "Of course!"

Peter Fargason

Adventurer 4, Discretionary Points 44, Medium-sized Human, HD 4d4+5, Hit Points 30, Energy Points 7, Initiative +0, Speed 30ft., AC 0 Base Attack +3, Fort +2, Ref +1, Will +2, Str 10 (0), Dex 10 (0), Con 12 (+1), Int 12 (+1), Wis 13 (+1), Cha 11 (0)

Attacks: +6 ranged (1d8+1, Concealable, Short Range, *Heavy Pistol*)

Attributes: Attack Combat Mastery 1, Aura of Command 4, Damn Healthy! 2, Defence Combat Mastery 1, Heightened Awareness 1, Highly Skilled 5, Personal Gear (Medium Pistol) 1, Organisational Ties (Hellsing) 4

Skills: Demolitions (Bomb Disposal) 2, Gun Combat (Pistol) 2, Heavy Weapons (Gunnery) 2,Intimidation (Political) 2, Knowledge: Military Sciences (Tactics) 2, Knowledge: Police Sciences (Forensics) 4, Knowledge: Occultism (Witchcraft) 1, Ranged Defence (Personal) 2, Unarmed Attack (Throws 2), Unarmed Defence (Holds) 1

Feats: Steady Hand, Weapon Encyclopaedia

Other Game Notes

Personal Gear

Peter always carries a medium semi-automatic pistol in a hip holster.

Organizational Ties

Peter is the head of military operations for the Hellsing Organization and the commanding officer of Company A. He takes orders directly from Integra.

JAN VALENTINE

Adventurer 9, Discretionary Points 44, Medium-sized Chipped Vampire, HD 9d4+18, Hit Points 61, Energy Points 13, Initiative +1, Speed 39ft., AC 4 (DCM +3, Dex +1), Base Attack +7/+2, Fort +5, Ref +4, Will +3, Str 14 (+2), Dex 13 (+1), Con 15 (+2), Int 10 (0), Wis 10 (0), Cha 14 (+2)

Attacks: +9, +4 ranged (1d6+1, Concealable, Short Range, Low Penetration, *Light Pistol*) or +7, +2 melee (1d8+2, Incapacitating, Drain Soul (Wisdom), Vampiric, Low Penetration, *Vampiric Bite*) or +8, +3 (1d8+1, Auto-fire, Spreading, Limited Shots (6), Short Range, *Submachine gun*)

Attributes: Attack Combat Mastery 3, Contamination (Ghoul or Vampire) 5, Damn Healthy! 2, Defence Combat Mastery 3, Feature (Longevity) 1, Magic (Vampiric) 4 [Mind Control (Created Ghouls) 5, Mind Control (Fearful Humans) 1, Regeneration 4], Natural Weapons (Fangs) 1, Organisational Ties (Freak Distribution) 2, Personal Gear (Guns) 1, Special Attack (Vampiric Bite) 4

Skills: Gun Combat (Pistol) 1, Heavy Weapons (Gunnery) 1, Intimidation (Street) 10, Open Lock (Electronic) 8, Ranged Defence (Personal) 2, Seduction (Female) 6

Feats: Accuracy, Two Weapon Fighting

Defects: Bane (Silver) 1, Bane (Sunlight) 2, Marked (Gold eyes, fangs and piercings) 2, Vampirism 1, Vulnerability (Fire) 1, Vulnerability (Silver) 1

OTHER GAME NOTES

ORGANIZATIONAL TIES

Jan is a member of a larger group responsible for the creation and distribution of the Freak chip. When Integra confronts Jan at the end of Episode 6 and asks who his master is, Jan sets himself on fire so that she'll be denied the information.

PERSONAL GEAR

Jan carries a medium pistol. He also owns a pair of submachine guns he uses during the siege of the Hellsing headquarters.

MARKED

Jan is easily recognized by his gold eyes and sharp fangs. He also has multiple facial piercings, including the eyebrow and lip, all with small gold hoops inserted.

LUKE VALENTINE

Adventurer 16, Discretionary Points 44, Medium-sized Chipped Vampire, HD 16d4+32, Hit Points 104, Energy Points 26, Initiative +7, Speed 48ft., AC 6 (DCM +3, Dex +3), Base Attack +11/+6/+1, Fort +7, Ref +8, Will +7, Str 14 (+2), Dex 16 (+3), Con 15 (+2), Int 14 (+2), Wis 15 (+2), Cha 16 (+3)

Attacks: +16, +16, +16, +16, +11, +6 ranged (2d6, Penetrating (Armour), Limited Shots (6), Short Range, *Customised shotgun*) or +11, +11, +11, +11, +6, +1 melee (1d8+2, Incapacitating, Drain Soul (Wisdom), Vampiric, Low Penetration, *Vampiric Bite*)

Attributes: Attack Combat Mastery 3, Aura of Command 2, Contamination (Ghoul or Vampire) 5, Damn Healthy! 3, Defence Combat Mastery 3, Extra Attacks 3, Feature (Longevity) 1, Heightened Awareness 1, Magic (Vampiric) 4 [Mind Control (Created Ghouls) 5, Mind Control (Fearful Humans) 1, Regeneration 4], Natural Weapons (Fangs) 1, Organisational Ties (Freak Distribution) 2, Personal Gear (Weapons) 2, Special Attack (Vampiric Bite) 4

Skills: Demolitions (Artificial Structures) 16, Gun Combat (Shotgun) 4, Intimidation (Interrogation) 16, Knowledge: Architecture (Fortifications) 9, Knowledge: Business (Small Business) 9, Knowledge: Military Sciences (Strategy) 16, Ranged Defence (Personal) 4

Feats: Improved Initiative, Steady Hand, Two Weapon Fighting

Defects: Bane (Silver) 1, Bane (Sunlight) 2, Marked (Red eyes, fangs) 1, Vampirism 1, Vulnerability (Fire) 1, Vulnerability (Silver) 2

OTHER GAME NOTES

ORGANIZATIONAL TIES

Luke is a member of a mysterious organization that supplied him and his brother with the Freak implants they wear. Their club is one of the distribution points for the Freak chips, as shown by the introduction to Episode 5.

PERSONAL GEAR

Luke's preferred weapons are two customised sawed-off shotguns firing slug ammunition — Damage 1d6, Penetrating (Armour), Limited Shots (6), Short Range). He typically wears them hidden under his jacket.

HARRY ANDERS

Adventurer 2, Discretionary Points 44, Medium-sized Human, HD 2d4+2, Hit Points 8, Energy Points 4, Initiative +1, Speed 36ft., AC 1 (Dex +1), Base Attack +1, Fort +1, Ref +1, Will +4, Str 10 (0), Dex 12 (+1), Con 12 (+1), Int 12 (+1), Wis 14 (+2), Cha 12 (+1)

Attacks: +4 (1d6, Unarmed Strike) or +4 ranged (1d6+1, Concealable, Short Range, *Light Pistol*)

Attributes: Aura of Command 2, Highly Skilled 6, Organisational Ties (MI-5) 2, Personal Gear (Pistol) 1

Skills: Gun Combat (Pistol) 2, Intimidation (Interrogation) 5, Knowledge: Military Sciences (Tactics) 5, Knowledge: Police Sciences (Criminology) 5, Melee Attack (Strikes) 2, Ranged Defence (Personal) 1, Wilderness Tracking (Urban) 4

Feats: Brawl, Iron Will, Judge Opponent, Point Blank Shot

Defects: Red Tape 1

OTHER GAME NOTES

PERSONAL GEAR

Harry always carries a medium semi-automatic pistol in a hip holster.

ORGANISATIONAL TIES

As a member of the MI-5 investigative unit, Harry has access to typical police resources — both physical and intelligence — and can call for backup as necessary.

RED TAPE

Harry must answer to a superior at MI-5, and is accountable for his actions while "on the clock." He is often required to fill out paperwork and jump through hoops before getting access to MI-5 resources.

SERGEANT PICKMAN

Adventurer 5, Discretionary Points 44, Medium-sized Human, HD 5d4+10, Hit Points 49, Energy Points 8, Initiative +1, Speed 36ft., AC 3 (DCM +2, Dex +1), Base Attack +4, Fort +5, Ref +2, Will +2, Str 14 (+2), Dex 12 (+1), Con 14 (+2), Int 12 (+1), Wis 12 (+1), Cha 10 (0)

Attacks: +4 (1d6+2, Unarmed Strike) or +7 ranged (1d8+1, Concealable, Short Range, *Heavy Pistol*) or +6 ranged (1d8+2, Auto-fire, Spreading, Limited Shots (6), *Assault Rifle*)

Attributes: Attack Combat Mastery 2, Aura of Command 3, Damn Healthy! 3, Defence Combat Mastery 2, Heightened Awareness 1, Highly Skilled 3, Organisational Ties (Hellsing) 2, Personal Gear (Weaponry) 1

Skills: Gun Combat (Pistol) 2, Heavy Weapons (Gunnery) 2, Intimidation (Interrogation) 2, Knowledge: Military Sciences (Tactics) 3, Knowledge: Occultism (Witchcraft) 2, Melee Attack (Strikes) 2, Ranged Defence (Personal) 2, Wilderness Tracking (Urban) 2

Feats: Accuracy, Brawl, Great Fortitude, Point Blank Shot

OTHER GAME NOTES

PERSONAL GEAR

Pickman always carries a medium semi-automatic pistol in a hip holster.

In addition, he has access (through Hellsing) to more powerful weaponry on assignment, most frequently a rifle.

ORGANISATIONAL TIES

Pickman is a Sergeant, leading one of the teams in Hellsing's first action squad.

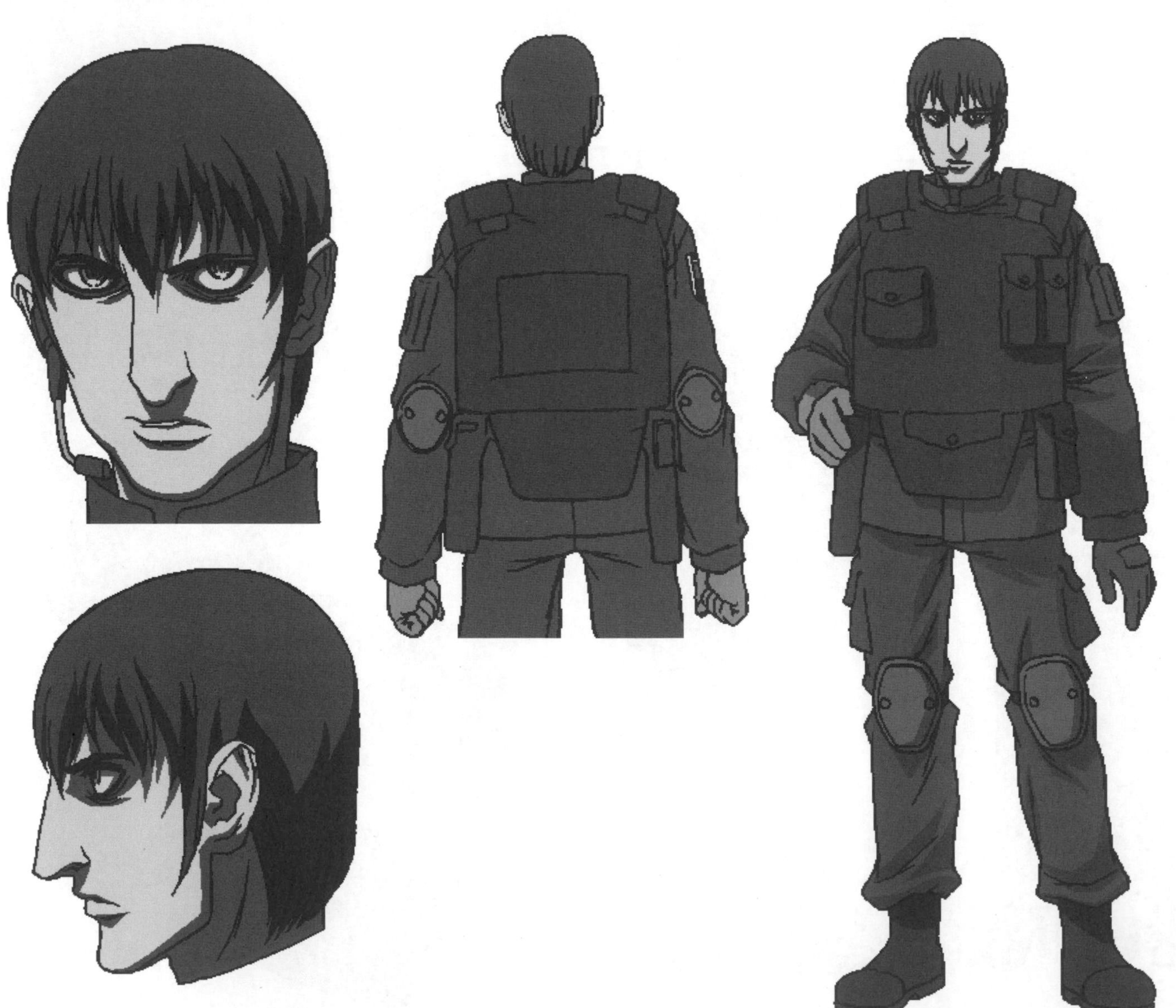

PAUL WILSON

Adventurer 11/Gun Bunny 2, Discretionary Points 44, Medium-sized Super Chipped Vampire, HD 11d4+33 plus 2d8+6, Hit Points 102, Energy Points 19, Initiative +6, Speed 42ft., AC 4 (DCM +2, Dex +2), Base Attack +9/+4, Fort +6, Ref +8, Will +4, Str 14 (+2), Dex 14 (+2), Con 16 (+3), Int 11 (0), Wis 13 (+1), Cha 12 (+1)

Attacks: +10, +5 melee (1d6+2, *Unarmed Strike*) or +9, +4 melee (1d8+2, Incapacitating, Drain Soul (Wisdom), Vampiric, Low Penetration, *Vampiric Bite*) or +16, +10 (1d8+1, Concealable, Short Range, *Heavy Pistol*)

Attributes: Attack Combat Mastery 2, Contamination (Ghoul or Vampire) 5, Damn Healthy! 2, Defence Combat Mastery 2, Divine Relationship 1, Feature (Longevity) 1, Highly Skilled 3, Magic (Vampiric) 7 [Alternate Form (Werewolf) 1, Insubstantial 4, Mind Control (Created Ghouls) 5, Mind Control (Fearful Humans) 1, Regeneration 4], Natural Weapons (Fangs) 1, Personal Gear (Pistol) 1, Special Attack (Vampiric Bite) 4

Skills: Gun Combat (Pistol) 6, Heavy Weapons (Gunnery) 2, Hide (Concealment) 4, Intimidation (Physical) 3, Knowledge: Military Sciences (Tactics) 5, Move Silently (Soft Step) 5, Navigate (Wilderness) 5, Ranged Defence (Personal) 4, Speak Language (Appropriate SAS Code) 1, Survival (Forest) 4, Tumble (Acrobatics) 4

Feats: Brawl, Improved Initiative, Leap Attack, Point Blank Shot

Defects: Bane (Silver) 1, Bane (Sunlight) 2, Marked (Red eyes, fangs) 1, Owned by Unknown Master Vampire 2, Vampirism 2, Vulnerability (Fire) 1, Vulnerability (Silver) 1, Wanted 2

OTHER GAME NOTES

Paul Wilson is the first of a new type of Freak chip vampire. Implanted with multiple chips under the supervision of Incognito, Wilson is able to shape change into a humanoid werewolf at will.

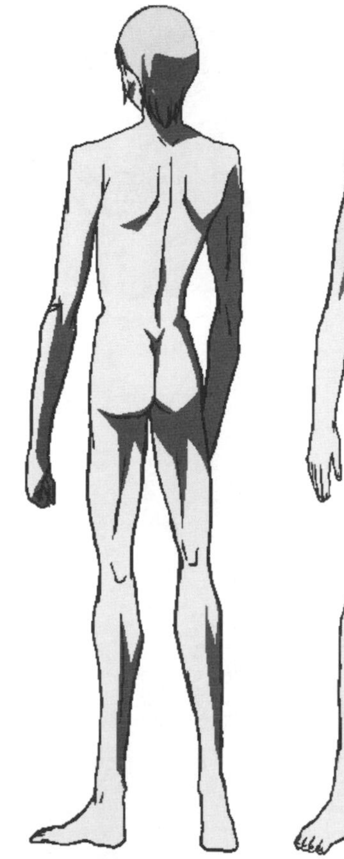

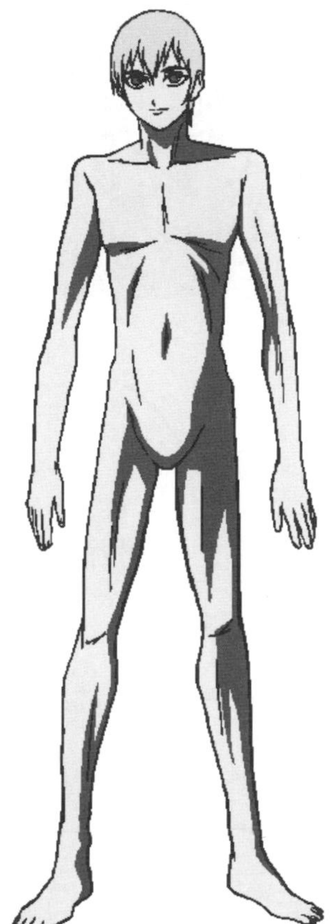

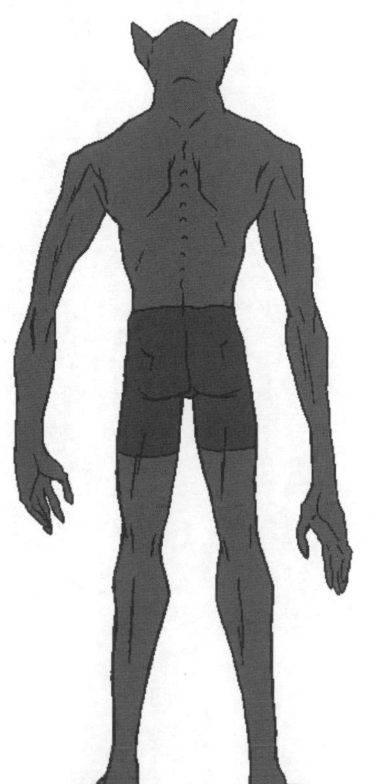

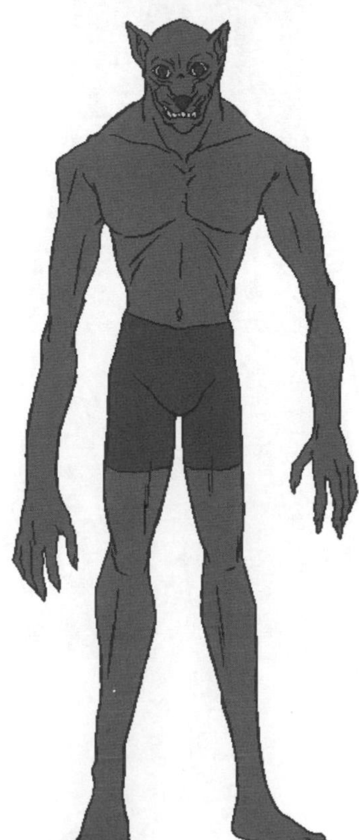

Laura / Boobhanshee

Adventurer 10, Discretionary Points 44, Medium-sized True Vampire, HD 10d4+10, Hit Points 54, Energy Points 16, Initiative +1, Speed 36ft., AC 4 (DCM +3, Dex +1), Base Attack +8/+3, Fort +4, Ref +3, Will +3, Str 14 (+2), Dex 12 (+1), Con 12 (+1), Int 12 (+1), Wis 11 (0), Cha 13 (+1)

Attacks: +9, +4 melee (1d6+2, *Unarmed Strike*) or +8, +3 melee (1d8+2, Incapacitating, Drain Soul (Wisdom), Vampiric, Low Penetration, *Vampiric Bite*)

Attributes: Attack Combat Mastery 3, Contamination (Ghoul or Vampire) 5, Damn Healthy! 2, Defence Combat Mastery 3, Feature (Longevity) 1, Heightened Senses (Vision) 1, Magic (Vampiric) 5 [Mind Control (Created Ghouls) 5, Mind Control (Humans) 3, Regeneration 4], Natural Weapons (Fangs) 1, Special Attack (Vampiric Bite) 4, Special Attack (Conversion Bite) 3, Super Strength 1

Skills: Bluff (Acting) 13, Hide (Skulking) 13, Knowledge: Occult (Spirits) 13, Move Silently (Soft Step) 13, Seduction (Female) 13

Feats: Brawl, Dodge

Defects: Bane (Silver) 1, Bane (Sunlight) 2, Marked (Red eyes, fangs) 1, Owned by Unknown Master Vampire 2, Vampirism 2, Vulnerability (Blessed weapons) 1, Vulnerability (Fire) 1, Vulnerability (Silver) 1

Other Game Notes

This writeup assumes that all of Laura's powers belong to her natively, and that neither Incognito nor anyone else directly aided her by transferring powers to her. Laura may have more powers than listed here, but did not exhibit any of them in *Hellsing* before Arucard killed her. In a *Hellsing d20* game set before her death, the GM may add an appropriate number of Attributes, Defects, and Skills to Laura to enhance her character.

Owned

While it is possible that Incognito is Laura's master, there is no direct evidence of this link. Nevertheless, this does not change the game effect of Owned; if you desire Laura to have a master that is not Incognito, simply create your own master for her and change the Attribute as appropriate.

Helena

Adventurer 19, Discretionary Points 44, Medium-sized True Vampire, HD 19d4+19, Hit Points 83, Energy Points 51, Initiative +1, Speed 36ft., AC 4 (DCM +3, Dex +1), Base Attack +12/+7/+2, Fort +7, Ref +7, Will +9, Str 14 (+2), Dex 12 (+1), Con 12 (+1), Int 16 (+3), Wis 16 (+3), Cha 18 (+4)

Attacks: +13, +8, +3 melee (1d6+2, Unarmed Strike) or +12, +7, +2 melee (1d8+2, Incapacitating, Drain Soul (Wisdom), Vampiric, Low Penetration, *Vampiric Bite*) or +12 ranged (5d8, Aura, Penetrating (Armour), Unique Attack Disability (Requires Teleportation), *Teleportation Attack*)

Attributes: Attack Combat Mastery 3, Contamination (Ghoul or Vampire) 5, Damn Healthy! 1, Defence Combat Mastery 3, Energy Bonus 2, Feature (Longevity) 1, Heightened Senses (Vision) 1, Magic (Vampiric) 4 [Mind Control (Created Ghouls) 5, Mind Control (Fearful Humans) 1, Regeneration 4], Natural Weapons (Fangs) 1, Special Attack (Vampiric Bite) 4, Special Attack (Conversion Bite) 3, Special Attack (Teleportation Attack) 6, Super Strength 1, Telepathy 4, Teleport 2

Skills: Bluff (Misdirection) 8, Decipher Script (Ancient Languages) 16, Diplomacy (Negotiation) 16, Gather Information (Contacts) 16, Investigate (Government) 8, Knowledge: Biological Sciences (Genetics) 20, Knowledge: Occult (Spirits) 22, Knowledge: Social Sciences (Anthropology) 20, Research (Historical) 17, Sense Motive (Mannerisms) 8

Feats: Brawl, Dodge

Defects: Bane (Silver) 1, Bane (Sunlight) 2, Marked (Red eyes, fangs) 1, Owned by Unknown Master Vampire 2, Unskilled 1, Vampirism 2, Vulnerability (Blessed weapons) 1, Vulnerability (Fire) 1, Vulnerability (Silver) 1

Other Game Notes

Helena appears to be a rather old and studied vampire; she almost certainly has more abilities than listed here. In a *BESM Hellsing* game set before her death, the GM may add an appropriate number of Attributes, Defects, and Skills to Helena to enhance her character.

Teleportation Attack

Helena's Teleportation Attack requires a Mind Stat check, and can only be done up to the "safe" distance, as listed in *Big Eyes, Small Mouth*. The character using this attack teleports "inside" the victim (ignoring size differences as necessary for dramatic effect) and then presses his or her way out of the victim, as if he or she was a tapeworm coming to the surface. If the attack fails, the character simply fails to teleport anywhere.

In *Hellsing,* Incognito counters this attack by simply cutting off Helena's head as she emerges from his stomach. Characters in *BESM Hellsing* may attempt to do the same with a Body + Mind ÷ 2 check — it takes both physical prowess and guts to cut off something that appears to be coming from within!

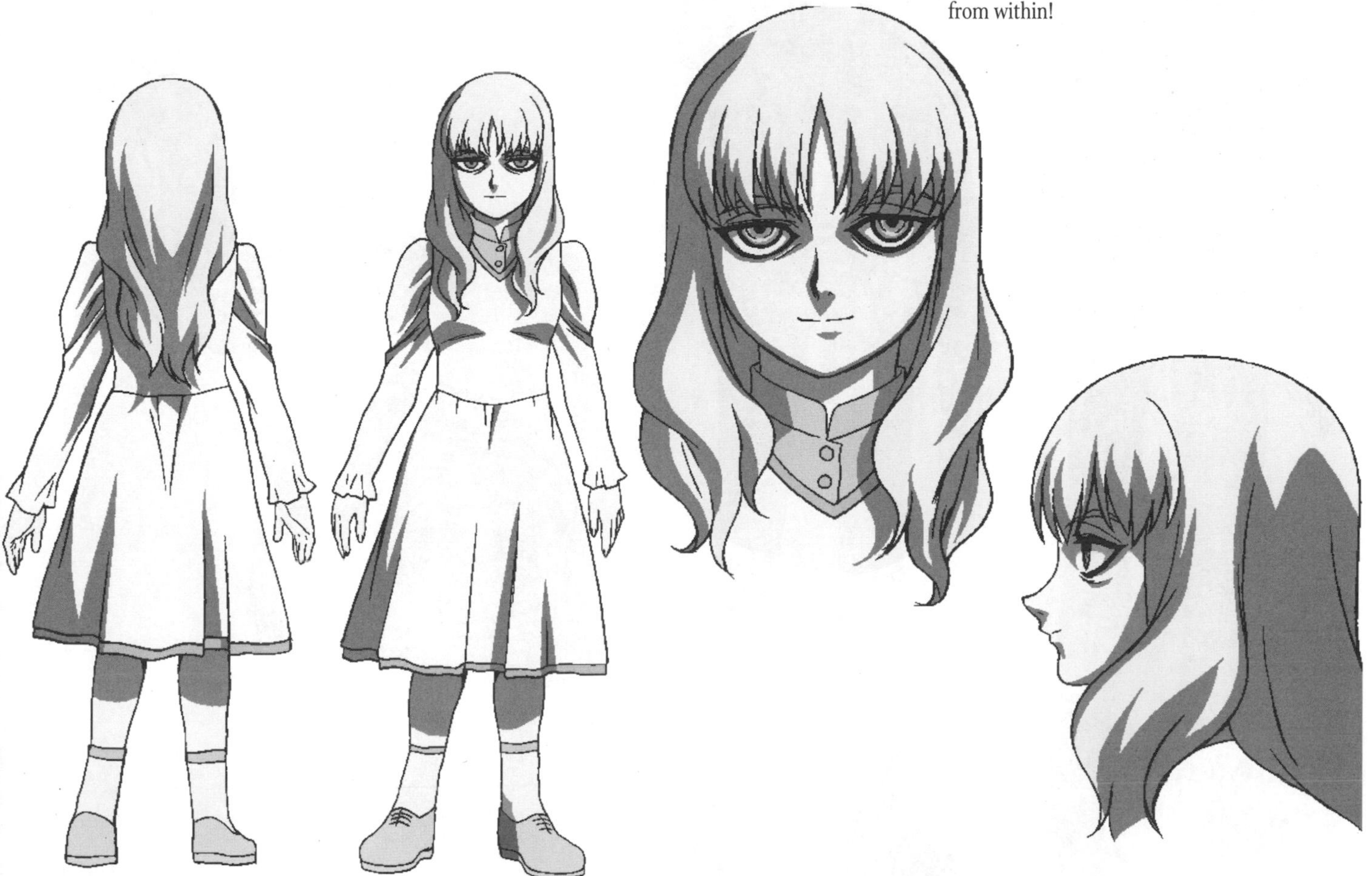

SIR HELLSING

Adventurer 5, Discretionary Points 44, Medium-sized Human, HD 5d4+5, Hit Points 34, Energy Points 10, Initiative +0, Speed 30ft., AC 0 Base Attack +2, Fort +2, Ref +1, Will +7, Str 10 (0), Dex 10 (0), Con 12 (+1), Int 16 (+3), Wis 18 (+4), Cha 16 (+3)

Attacks: +7 ranged (1d8+1, Concealable, Short Range, *Heavy Pistol*)

Attributes: Aura of Command 3, Damn Healthy! 2, Highly Skilled 3, Organisational Ties (Hellsing) 5, Unique Attribute (Sleeping Alucard) 1

Skills: Gather Information (Contacts) 4, Gun Combat (Pistol) 4, Intimidation (Political) 8, Investigate (Government) 4, Knowledge: Business (Executive) 8, Knowledge: Military Sciences (Intelligence Analysis) 7, Knowledge: Police Sciences (Criminology) 8, Knowledge: Occultism (Witchcraft) 8, Research (Legal) 4

Feats: Judge Opponent, Iron Will, Point Blank Shot

Defects: Nemesis (Richard Hellsing) 2

BACKGROUND

SLEEPING ARUCARD

The vampire Arucard is restrained in the Hellsing Mansion basement until after Sir Hellsing's death. In a *Hellsing d20* game set before the death of Sir Hellsing, the resting Arucard is obviously an "ace in the hole" that could be woken up by Sir Hellsing or discovered by another character (as Integra did).

NEMESIS

Richard Hellsing is Sir Hellsing's Nemesis, even though he does not reveal his plot to usurp control of the Hellsing Organisation until after Sir Hellsing dies. In a *Hellsing d20* campaign set before the death of Sir Hellsing, Richard would subtly interfere and manipulate events to make Sir Hellsing look less competent as he builds toward taking control of the Hellsing Organisation.

Richard Hellsing

Adventurer 2, Discretionary Points 44, Medium-sized Human, HD 2d4, Hit Points 18, Energy Points 5, Initiative +0, Speed 33ft., AC 0, Base Attack +2, Fort +0, Ref +0, Will +5, Str 10 (0), Dex 11 (0), Con 11 (0), Int 14 (+2), Wis 12 (+1), Cha 12 (+1)

Attacks: +4 (1d6, Unarmed Strike) or +5 ranged (1d8+1, Concealable, Short Range, *Heavy Pistol*)

Attributes: Attack Combat Mastery 1, Damn Healthy! 2, Flunkies 3, Highly Skilled 2, Organisational Ties (Hellsing) 1, Personal Gear (Pistol and weaponry) 2

Skills: Gun Combat (Pistol) 2, Intimidation (Interrogation) 4, Knowledge: Business (Executive) 4, Knowledge: Military Sciences (Intelligence Analysis) 4, Knowledge: Police Sciences (Criminology) 4, Knowledge: Occultism (Witchcraft) 4, Unarmed Attack (Strikes) 1

Feats: Accuracy, Brawl, Iron Will, Point Blank Shot

Background

Flunkies

Richard has 4 goons/bodyguards at his disposal. Treat them as statistically identical to Richard, but remove the following Attributes: Flunkies and Organisational Ties and any related skills.

Organisational Ties

It is unknown exactly what level of status Richard Hellsing carries in the Hellsing Organisation.

Personal Gear

Richard carries a pistol, but has access to superior equipment through Hellsing. It is also likely that over time he has surreptitiously stolen equipment from Hellsing to arm his flunkies.

CAST

Arucard	George Nakata (Japanese) Crispin Freeman (English)
Integra	Yoshiko Sakakibara (Japanese) Victoria Harwood (English)
Seras	Fumiko Orikasa (Japanese) K.T. Grey (English)
Walter	Motomu Kiyokawa (Japanese) Ralph Lister (English)
Andersong	Nachi Nozawa (Japanese) Steven Brand (English)
Peter Fargason	Unsho Ishizuka (Japanese)
Gareth	Tomoyuki Shimura (Japanese) Peter Gail (English)

Scriptwriter	Chiaki J. Konaka
Storyboard/Director	Yasunori Urata
Animation Director	Toshiharu Murata
Key Animators	Toshiharu Murata Reichi Sasajima Yoshitaka Kono Shinobu Tagashira Yuji Hosogoe Yusuke Yoshigaki Hiroyuki Horiuchi Mitsuru Obunai Seiji Masuda Hiroshi Mimata Miwako Yamamoto Fumitoshi Oizaki Hideyuki Yoshida
Background Art	Green Takashi Aoi Norifumi Nakamura Miyoko Kohama Eri Nakamura
Colour Coordinator/ Colour Checker	Takae Iijima
Digital Retoucher	Shin Inoie
Animation Checker	Yasunori Matsumura
Animators	Yasunori Matsumura Kind Production Mi Dr. Movie
Digital Painters	T2 Studio Dr. Movie
Digital Compositors	Atsushi Takeyama Amga Naoyuki Taniguchi Mizue Honmiya Yuki Okada
Sound Effects	Kouji Kasamatsu
Sound Regulator	Shoji Hata
Sound Assistant	Fumaiki Tanaka
Sound Effects Manager	Yoshimi Sugiyama

OPENING ANIMATION STAFF

Storyboard	Yoshikazu Miyao
Directors	Yoshikazu Miyao Yasunori Urata
Animation Director	Toshiharu Murata
Key Animators	Asago Akiko Shinobu Tagashira Yoshiyuki Ito Hiroyuki Imaishi Yusuke Yoshigaki Tatsuya Oka Kazuo Sakai Yuji Hosogoe Toshiharu Murata
Digital Effects	Masaya Suzuki
Digital Retoucher	Ishin Inoie
Opening Theme	"Cool†-The World without Logos"
Performed by	Yasushi Ishii
Lyrics and Composition	Yasushi Ishii (Pioneer LDC)

ENDING ANIMATION STAFF

Storyboard	Umanosuke Iida
Director	Yasunori Urata
Key Animators	Yoshitaka Kono Toshiharu Murata
3D CG	Teitoku Kaneda
Digital Colouring	Keiko Kai Takae Iijima
Digital Retoucher	Ishin Inoie
Ending Theme	"Shine"
Performed by	Mr. Big
Written by	Riche Kotzen/Richie Ziti (East West Japan)

Music Producer	Toshiaki Ohta (Border Line)
Music Support	East West Japan Fujipacific Music Inc.
Logo & Design Works	Norihiko Nezu G-Square
Weapons Technical Support	Dainihongiken
Format Editors	Toshikazu Doko Osamu Takagi (Sony PCL)
Assistant Producer	Mie Ide (Pioneer LDC)
Production Manager	Koji Kajita
Line Producers	Manabu Ishikawa Takahiko Sakagami
Assistant Production Manager	Masashi Otokawa
Public Relations	Takashi Iida (Pioneer LDC) Keiko Tabata (Gonzo) Yuko Fujita (Gonzo)
TV Public Relations	Tadanobu Inaba (Fuji Television)
Production Support	Akihiro Yuasa (Sotsu Agency Co., LTD.)
Executive Producers	Yoshinori Kumazawa (Pioneer LDC) Akihiro Kawamura (Pioneer LDC) Shinichiro Ishikawa Yosuke Kobayashi (Pioneer Entertainment USA) Hideki Goto (Pioneer Entertainment USA)
Produced by	Hellsing K. G. Fuji Television
English Version Produced by	Pioneer Entertainment (USA) Inc.
In Association With	New Generation Pictures
Executive Producer	Hideki "Henry" Goto
Producers	Hiroe Tsukamoto Satoshi Fujii Reiko Matsuo Jonathan Klein
Voice Director	Taliesin Jaffe
Translation	Reiko Matsuo
ADR Script Editors	Taliesin Jaffe Jonathan Klein
DVD Subtitlers	Brett Jacobsen Aki Matsumoto Makoto Shirai Diana Tolin
Audio Recording & Video Editing Facilities Provided by	The Post Office, LLC.
Recording Engineer/ Sound Mixer	Sean Vahle
Video Editor	Chris Ladegaard

#4
セラス私服
2001. 9 by T. MURATA
18発
HELLSHING
HALCONNEN 30mm
ANTI MIDIANS CANNON
D.U. shell
MEDICAL
BLOOD
TYPE
A
RH

REVISED EDITION

besm d20

anime role-player's handbook

Available now in all fine hobby stores or visit http://www.guardiansorder.com.

'd20 System' and the d20 System logo are trademarks of Wizards of the Coast, Inc. in the United States and other countries and are used with permission.

d20
system
d20 mecha
The d20 System Mecha Handbook

TRIGUN
d20
system

A

B

C

D

E

F

G

H

I

J

K

L

M

N

O

P

R

S

T

U

V

W

OPEN GAME LICENSE Version 1.0a

The following text is the property of Wizards of the Coast, Inc. and is Copyright 2000 Wizards of the Coast, Inc ("Wizards"). All Rights Reserved.

1. Definitions: (a)"Contributors" means the copyright and/or trademark owners who have contributed Open Game Content; (b)"Derivative Material" means copyrighted material including derivative works and translations (including into other computer languages), potation, modification, correction, addition, extension, upgrade, improvement, compilation, abridgment or other form in which an existing work may be recast, transformed or adapted; (c) "Distribute" means to reproduce, license, rent, lease, sell, broadcast, publicly display, transmit or otherwise distribute; (d)"Open Game Content" means the game mechanic and includes the methods, procedures, processes and routines to the extent such content does not embody the Product Identity and is an enhancement over the prior art and any additional content clearly identified as Open Game Content by the Contributor, and means any work covered by this License, including translations and derivative works under copyright law, but specifically excludes Product Identity. (e) "Product Identity" means product and product line names, logos and identifying marks including trade dress; artifacts; creatures characters; stories, storylines, plots, thematic elements, dialogue, incidents, language, artwork, symbols, designs, depictions, likenesses, formats, poses, concepts, themes and graphic, photographic and other visual or audio representations; names and descriptions of characters, spells, enchantments, personalities, teams, personas, likenesses and special abilities; places, locations, environments, creatures, equipment, magical or supernatural abilities or effects, logos, symbols, or graphic designs; and any other trademark or registered trademark clearly identified as Product identity by the owner of the Product Identity, and which specifically excludes the Open Game Content; (f) "Trademark" means the logos, names, mark, sign, motto, designs that are used by a Contributor to identify itself or its products or the associated products contributed to the Open Game License by the Contributor (g) "Use", "Used" or "Using" means to use, Distribute, copy, edit, format, modify, translate and otherwise create Derivative Material of Open Game Content. (h) "You" or "Your" means the licensee in terms of this agreement.

2. The License: This License applies to any Open Game Content that contains a notice indicating that the Open Game Content may only be Used under and in terms of this License. You must affix such a notice to any Open Game Content that you Use. No terms may be added to or subtracted from this License except as described by the License itself. No other terms or conditions may be applied to any Open Game Content distributed using this License.

3. Offer and Acceptance: By Using the Open Game Content You indicate Your acceptance of the terms of this License.

4. Grant and Consideration: In consideration for agreeing to use this License, the Contributors grant You a perpetual, worldwide, royalty-free, non-exclusive license with the exact terms of this License to Use, the Open Game Content.

5. Representation of Authority to Contribute: If You are contributing original material as Open Game Content, You represent that Your Contributions are Your original creation and/or You have sufficient rights to grant the rights conveyed by this License.

6. Notice of License Copyright: You must update the COPYRIGHT NOTICE portion of this License to include the exact text of the COPYRIGHT NOTICE of any Open Game Content You are copying, modifying or distributing, and You must add the title, the copyright date, and the copyright holder's name to the COPYRIGHT NOTICE of any original Open Game Content you Distribute.

7. Use of Product Identity: You agree not to Use any Product Identity, including as an indication as to compatibility, except as expressly licensed in another, independent Agreement with the owner of each element of that Product Identity. You agree not to indicate compatibility or co-adaptability with any Trademark or Registered Trademark in conjunction with a work containing Open Game Content except as expressly licensed in another, independent Agreement with the owner of such Trademark or Registered Trademark. The use of any Product Identity in Open Game Content does not constitute a challenge to the ownership of that Product Identity. The owner of any Product Identity used in Open Game Content shall retain all rights, title and interest in and to that Product Identity.

8. Identification: If you distribute Open Game Content You must clearly indicate which portions of the work that you are distributing are Open Game Content.

9. Updating the License: Wizards or its designated Agents may publish updated versions of this License. You may use any authorized version of this License to copy, modify and distribute any Open Game Content originally distributed under any version of this License.

10. Copy of this License: You MUST include a copy of this License with every copy of the Open Game Content You Distribute.

11. Use of Contributor Credits: You may not market or advertise the Open Game Content using the name of any Contributor unless You have written permission from the Contributor to do so.

12. Inability to Comply: If it is impossible for You to comply with any of the terms of this License with respect to some or all of the Open Game Content due to statute, judicial order, or governmental regulation then You may not Use any Open Game Material so affected.

13. Termination: This License will terminate automatically if You fail to comply with all terms herein and fail to cure such breach within 30 days of becoming aware of the breach. All sublicenses shall survive the termination of this License.

14. Reformation: If any provision of this License is held to be unenforceable, such provision shall be reformed only to the extent necessary to make it enforceable.

15. COPYRIGHT NOTICE

Open Game License v 1.0a Copyright 2000, Wizards of the Coast, Inc.

System Rules Document Copyright 2000, Wizards of the Coast, Inc.; Authors Jonathan Tweet, Monte Cook, Skip Williams, based on original material by E. Gary Gygax and Dave Arneson.

Modern System Reference Document Copyright 2002, Wizards of the Coast, Inc.; Authors Bill Slavicsek, Jeff Grubb, Rich Redman, Charles Ryan, based on material by Jonathan Tweet, Monte Cook, Skip Williams, Richard Baker, Peter Adkison, Bruce R. Cordell, John Tynes, Andy Collins, and JD Wiker.

Silver Age Sentinels d20 Copyright 2002, Guardians of Order, Inc.; Authors Stephen Kenson, Mark C. MacKinnon, Jeff Mackintosh, Jesse Scoble.

BESM d20 Copyright 2003, Guardians of Order, Inc.; Author Mark C. MacKinnon.

Hellsing d20 Copyright 2004, Guardians of Order, Inc; Authors Adam Jury, Matthew Keeley, Michelle Lyons

DESIGNATION OF PRODUCT IDENTITY

The following is designated as Product Identity, in accordance with Section 1(e) of the Open Game License, Version 1.0a: All Guardians Of Order names, logos, identifying marks, and trade dress; all character, creation, vehicle, and place names; all examples, all artwork, symbols, designs, depictions, illustrations, likenesses, poses, and graphic design; all stories, storylines, plots, thematic elements, and dialogue; pages 1-112.

DESIGNATION OF OPEN GAME CONTENT

Subject to the Product Identity designation above, the remainder of this publication is designated as Open Game Content.